2 -

BY CHELSEA HANDLER

My Horizontal Life

Are You There, Vodka? It's Me, Chelsea

Lies That Chelsea Handler Told Me

Chelsea Chelsea Bang Bang

Uganda Be Kidding Me

Life Will Be the Death of Me

LIFE
WILL BE
THE
DEATH
OF ME

LIFE WILL BE THE D⊿ATH OF ME

...AND YOU TOO!

Chelsea Handler

SPIEGEL & GRAU
New York

To My Future Husband, With Love

Far too many people are looking for

the right person, instead of trying to be

the right person.

—GLORIA STEINEM

CONTENTS

LIFE
WILL BE
THE
D忆ATH
OF ME

WHERE
HAVE
I BEEN
ALL MY
LIFE

I don't remember the actor, and I don't remember the movie, but I remember it was five o'clock in the afternoon and I had just taken a couple hits off my vape pen. I needed to load my Pix account, which held pre-released movies that I was expected to screen before a star of one of the movies was a guest on my Netflix talk show. I was sitting on one of my overpriced chaise longues, the kind that celebrities and Russians purchase for their bedrooms, when I found myself once again unable to convert the TV that descends from the ceiling from Apple TV to Pix. Rich people have descending smart televisions. The idea is that they descend silently and gracefully from the ceiling, but because I am nouveau-riche rich, mine sounds more like a helicopter landing. I'd like to blame my inability to change the mode of my television to Pix on the fact that I was stoned, but that would be a lie; I'd be even less capable if I was sober.

I called my assistant Brandon at his house, to tell him to tell my other assistant, Tanner—who was downstairs in my house—to come upstairs and help me with the television. I hung up the phone. I looked down at the table and saw the vape pen. *How many more hits of marijuana would I need to get through this movie?*

I knew things had hit a new low—or high, depending on how you looked at the situation. I picked up the iPad that controls the TV along with everything else in my house—from the window shades to the exterior lights in my backyard, to my pulse, probably—and tried to pretend that I was troubleshooting, so that Tanner would think I had at least tried to figure it out on my own—*as if that had ever happened before.*

How did I become so useless? And how many assistants did I actually have? Answer: two. Brandon and Tanner. Brandon is gay and has an incredible attention to detail. Tanner is straight, and before he met me, he thought the Four Seasons was a weather pattern. Before I met Tanner, I thought Venmo was an online liquor store.

Tanner was now upstairs standing behind the chaise I was sitting on. I wondered if he could smell the weed I'd just smoked, and if so, what did he think of me? Did he realize that most television hosts don't even make the time to watch movies and TV shows to prepare for each of their upcoming guests? Did he understand that I was a consummate professional who went to great lengths to get ready for my show? Or did he think that I was just some rich, lucky, white bitch who continued to fall upward? No, that wasn't quite right: I doubt he was thinking in terms of race. Two white people surely weren't thinking about skin color. I was the one thinking that.

I didn't want to watch another stupid fucking movie that I didn't care about. And I really didn't want to interview another action star bloviating about his motivation for playing a half man, half mermaid. I just didn't care, and I wasn't doing anyone any favors by pretending that I did.

Did I ever care? The answer is yes. There was a time when all of this mattered to me. There was a time when being famous and having this kind of success and money and having a TV show was what drove me to want more and more and more, and now I found myself exhausted and ashamed by the meaninglessness of it all.

I remember coming home a couple of weeks before the 2016 election on a windy fall night—which for Los Angeles is rare. Anytime there's weather in Los Angeles, even rain, it's exciting—the constant sunshine can start to grate on your nerves. I went up to my bedroom, opened up my sliding glass doors, grabbed my vape pen, and turned on some Neil Young. I lay on my bed in the dark, watching the wind blow my bedroom drapes around, hearing the ruffling of the leaves, and watching the lanterns that hang from my backyard trees swinging into each other, thinking, *If there's an electrical fire, I hope the dogs will at least bark to wake me up,* but overall, my thought was: *This is fucking awesome. This is exactly what I'd hoped adulthood would be.*

No kids, no husband, no responsibilities—just a TV show on Netflix and whatever else I felt like doing, whenever I felt like doing it. Not trapped, not stuck, not dependent on a single person but myself—free to be you and me. I couldn't believe how lucky my life had turned out, how many of my dreams had come true, and also my good fortune in being alive during this time in history—the year we were going to elect our first female president.

I suppose I could blame my state of mind on the election of Donald Trump—so I will. I have the Trump family and their horrifying personalities and veneers to thank for my midlife crisis. Along with more than half the population—of the world—I couldn't grasp how, in this day and age, we elected a man who insulted Mexicans and women and Muslims and veterans and disabled people and everyone else he has insulted since. The contrast in decency between Barack Obama and Donald Trump was too much for me to bear—like electing Snooki to the Senate. Now people were seriously talking about Dwayne "the Rock" Johnson running for president. How on earth did we get here? Although, if I'm being honest, at that point in time—or at any other time during the entire Trump presidency—I would have preferred an *actual* rock.

How could Americans have turned their back on decency, and why was I so misinformed? How did I not know this outcome was even a possibility? *What was I missing?*

I kept hearing the word "elitists"—that everyone in California and New York lived in a bubble. That the election of this lunatic was a result of all of us not knowing anything about the rest of the country.

That didn't ring true for me. I had traveled all over the country doing stand-up for so many years. I had been to every major and some minor cities multiple times. I wasn't an elitist. My father was a used-car dealer. I didn't have a trust fund or wealthy parents. We weren't allowed to answer the phone growing up because, more often than not, it would be a bill collector. I had four hundred dollars when I drove across the country alone to move to Los Angeles, and then was broke for seven years living paycheck to paycheck, while simultaneously getting fired from every waitressing job I ever had. I worked for everything I have and never even went to college. *How could I be an elitist without ever having gone to college?*

And then—*Oh, wait a minute, now I remember.*

I grew up wanting to get as far away from the life my parents had given me as possible. I had created a life in which there was a zero-tolerance policy for any discomfort. I could handle physical discomfort, like dental work or elective surgery to make my thighs smaller, but not any discomfort related to not having money.

Sure, I was just scraping by on those cross-country trips in the beginning of my stand-up career, barely making enough money from small comedy clubs to cover my hotel room for the week. But after a few years, I was earning more money—and the clubs turned into theaters, then arenas, with private planes and chauffeured cars, sometimes for less than twenty-four hours and then on to the next city, so here I was again, not taking into account the optics—or for that matter, the reality—of my own entitlement.

I had become exactly what I'd always wanted to be—an elitist.

I did live in a bubble, inside a bigger bubble, which was inside an even bigger bubble. Three bubbles. Two assistants, two cleaning ladies (who are more like my nannies), a driver, a pool guy, a landscaper, a florist, a houseman. What is a houseman, you ask? Someone who walks the dogs and polishes the outdoor furniture, and, oh, cleans up the dog shit outside. Basically, an outdoor butler. When was the last time I cleaned up dog shit? Probably the last time I flew coach.

I hated having these thoughts. I hated it because something clicked in the process of making these associative leaps. I realized that I'd made a career of over-hydrating people with my honesty, yet I was being dishonest with myself, which left me operating in a deficit of truth. Now that I was aware of this situation, I would have to do something about it. I couldn't carry on the way I had been carrying on, just coasting and cashing checks for essentially being a loudmouth.

I took another hit of my vape.

. . .

What I *really* wanted to do was watch the news, even though the news was giving me diarrhea. The whole administration was giving me diarrhea. My outrage was high. I had spent the year after the election being sucked into the vortex of news cycles that accompanied Donald Trump's ascendancy and my subsequent mental hernia. The news was like a high-speed merry-go-round that never slowed down long enough to figure out when it was safe to hop on or off, so like everything in my life thus far, I hopped on and stayed on.

I had spent the better part of my day in a wormhole,

googling pictures of "young Robert Mueller" because I was developing strong sexual feelings toward him as well as his investigation. In an interesting plot twist, it turns out Bob Mueller is even hotter in his early seventies than he was when he was in the Marines. I was more attracted to present-day Bob Mueller than I would have been had I been alive during 'Nam. The guy fucking kills me. Who is hotter than Bob Mueller? Daniel Day-Lewis playing Bob Mueller, maybe, but the jury is out until that movie is released and Daniel Day-Lewis gives up "shoe cobbling" for a year. *I mean, my God. Just stop it with the cobbling. Just act. You're great at it. People adore you. No one's talking about your shoes. Maybe your wife, but I doubt it.*

Bob Mueller was the only hope I had that Donald Trump and that terrible vampire family he spawned would end up in prison. The investigation into Donald Trump and his conspiring with Russia and all the other crimes I'm sure he'll be indicted for made me realize what real men look like. They look like Bob Mueller. A seventy-four-year-old with a six-pack (possibly an eight-pack) underneath that suit. You can see it through his shirt when he walks—he's ripped. "Keeping your shit together" is what that's called. A prosecutor, a Marine, and the director of the FBI? How on earth is any woman worth her salt meant to control herself around him and not sit directly on his face? And then, that hair-part? Very few seventy-year-old men have a head of hair like that, and if anyone knows their way around seventy-year-old men, it's me—they're my core demographic. The thickness . . . the salt and pepper . . . it's one thing after another with this patriot.

My best friend, Mary, and I have spent many a night deliberating about what he drinks when he gets home after a long day. Was it a scotch on the rocks . . . or a scotch neat?

"One ice cube," Mary would say. "And it would be Macallan." People who use one ice cube usually annoy me, but this was different. I knew that Bob Mueller knew better than I did, and if he wanted to use one ice cube, then he was trying to accomplish something different with his libation—something that only a scotch or whiskey drinker knew about. I would be willing to switch over to scotch or whiskey—and even use one ice cube for the rest of my life—if the reward meant seeing Donald Trump dragged out of the White House topless, handcuffed, in his tighty-whiteys, while his hairpiece detached from the tape on his head and flew around like a cyclone, landing in the Rose Garden.

. . .

On the subject of ice—once we sort out this Donald Trump situation, I would like my social activism to focus solely on the integrity of ice.

Temperature and ice are two of my most learned subject matters.

I feel strongly that everybody needs to get on the same page with ice. It's an international issue, and there aren't enough people taking it seriously. Just like there's an appropriate glass for every libation, there is an appropriate amount of ice as well. It's called, *Whatever you're thinking—double it.* If you've ever been to Europe, then you know what I'm talking about. No one wants a warm cocktail, and the only reason Europeans tolerate the ice situation there is because ice is not high on the European Union's list of priorities.

Two ice cubes in a mixed-drink glass do not even begin to cool your drink. The fewer the ice cubes, the less consolidation the ice has—therefore, you may as well just add water. If anyone wanted a vodka and soda with a splash of water, it would be its own thing by now. Cocktails should be cold. Cubes. Plural. Not the rapper.

Mary's ice in her freezer always has corn mixed in it. She says it's because she has three little girls, but I don't see how that correlates to corn in her ice maker. Anyway, when I go to Mary's, I always have a vodka with corn on the rocks. She says that the ice and corn are both frozen and that I should just think of the corn as extra ice.

. . .

I'm not embarrassed by my feelings for Robert Mueller. Surprised, maybe—but not embarrassed. I am legitimately attracted to him and everything he stands for. I respect the shit out of him, and I suspect there will be a lot of people naming their baby boys Bob after this whole shitshow is over. Who would have thought a name like Bob would finally take off?

"Boxers or briefs?" I asked. Mary was aghast.

"Chelsea, Bob Mueller is a Marine. Boxers, *obviously*, and don't think for a second he's not also wearing a Fruit of the Loom undershirt to sleep in as well. Snug and tidy. That's how Marines like it."

"A wifebeater? Those ribbed ones? Like what gang members wear?"

"No, dummy. He's not rolling his face off on molly in Ibiza. It's a crew neck Fruit of the Loom undershirt—short-sleeved. Think Hanes for men. Bob Mueller is not wearing a fucking tank top."

Mary's father was a Marine and Mary knows more than I do regarding just about everything (unless of course I tell her about something—like a diet—that she dismisses and then finds out about it months later from another friend and tells me about it like I wasn't the one who told her about it in the first place), so more often than not, I defer to her, and I had to accept these musings as cold, hard facts. The only thing I knew about Marines was that they had a strong relationship with water—which, it turns out, they don't. That's the Navy. My thoughts were as follows: marine life = sea life, Marines = water army. I'm a literal thinker—at least that's what my new psychiatrist tells me . . . or what I tell him.

"*Semper fi* is a term that Marines use that means 'always faithful,'" I told Mary. "It's the motto of the United States Marines. How hot is that?"

"Yes, I know that, and please don't start throwing that term around. One, you're not Latin, and two, you're not a Marine."

"Copy that," I told her, knowing full well I would be adding *semper fi* to my rotation of words and phrases that no one has used in fifty years.

"You know he still does push-ups every morning and never eats unless it's for fuel," Mary added, twirling her hair. "He's *that* guy."

"It's all so fucking hot," I said, scouring her liquor cabinet for some Macallan, eager to see how it would taste with frozen corn.

Imagining Bob Mueller sitting in his boxers and a little boy's Hanes undershirt with short sleeves while drinking Macallan on the rock—probably in a leather club chair—made me feel like Bob Mueller and I had a lot more in common than anyone would guess, even me. I imagined us playing Clue together in a cozy cabin in the Catskills, learning entirely new strategies to a game I thought I had already intellectually mastered. I understand Bob Mueller is married and unavailable, so I would like to go on the record and say I respect that—while also remaining deeply attracted to him. It wouldn't matter if he was interested in me or not; I don't need people to like me in order for me to like them. That's a new philosophy I've been toying with, and I like it.

Through the months of thick fog and despair after the election, he was the one bright spot. He also represented a seminal moment for me personally; I had finally found the first Republican I could see myself being penetrated by. #MuellerTime.

· · ·

Back to my midlife crisis. There is a line I had written down from Viktor Frankl's memoir about surviving the Holocaust, *Man's Search for Meaning*, that stopped me cold when I read it: "it did not really matter what we expected from life, but rather what life expected from us." I had never thought about what life expected from me. I had only thought about what I expected from life. That was a book putter-downer.

It was a look up at the sky and wonder *Where the fuck have I been all my life?* moment.

My dad used to tell me that there was always one line in every book that summed up the entire book. He also said that even if you don't understand everything you're reading in an article or a book, or even hearing in a conversation, try to take one piece of information away from it—that way you've left with something new to add to your brain. At the time, I was only eight, but I was already sick and tired of my father forcing me to read so many hard books—*The Fountainhead, East of Eden, Anna Karenina*—that I would always look for the first line that I thought would give him the impression that I had read the books he assigned. This was that line from Viktor Frankl. *What does life expect out of me?*

How lost was I if that question had never occurred to me—and it hadn't. I had to read it to think it. What a fucking dummy I was, rewarding myself over and over again with homes and cars and vacations and gross extravagance. I justified all of it because I worked for everything I had. *I came from nothing*, I told myself. For years, that was my story. *Work hard, fight hard, don't give up. You can do anything. You deserve this.*

The idea that I came from nothing is a joke. My parents were disappointing in many respects, but I always felt loved—by a lot of people. I never went hungry. I never struggled. I was white, pretty, and Jewish, and had a ton of misplaced self-confidence, so life got easier the more focused I became. I got to Hollywood and was rewarded for all of the above. It took a few years, but I never thought it wasn't going to happen, and people who like me can say it's because of talent, but talent is a nonissue. There are too many untalented people who are successful, and too many talented people who aren't. Talent is neither here nor there. Becoming famous just seemed like the easiest way to become wealthy without going to college. That was my mindset. It was a lot of luck and a lot of privilege.

My life *was* a bubble. That's exactly what it had become. A big vapid bubble. What were my ties to being famous? To being a celebrity? Wealth and fame existed as a couple in my mind; they went together. *Did that mean I could still have one without the other—and, if so, which one would I choose? Was this my whole life?* No. It can't be.

Do I get to fall in love again? With a man? No, a man can't help me with this. You got yourself here. So, the question is: *What am I going to do with myself now? What is my enough?*

I've always been generous, but that's always come easily to me. It's easy to give. If anything, it feeds my ego to give to others. Real generosity is also showing up when you *don't* feel like it—sacrificing your own happiness in exchange for someone else's. Was I willing to do that? What am I willing to do that I really don't want to do? *Is that something I'm even capable of?*

I never had to care about the state of the world before. The world was a vague thought and a whimsical fancy—that was for the adults. I thought that by traveling to so many different countries, I was doing my due diligence, that by edifying myself with other cultures, and sharing my experiences on camera and on my show, I was somehow making a worthy contribution to society. America wasn't a problem. There was no problem. We had elected a black president. Racism and feminism were fights we had already won. America was being handled by people smarter and more skilled in politics, and they took care of this stuff so that people like me could live the American dream and remain blissfully ill-informed. I had spent my adulthood on a cigarette boat going a hundred miles per hour, and now I felt like I had somehow become marooned on one of those terrible all-inclusive Carnival cruise ships.

• • •

Tanner fixed my TV and awkwardly put the iPad on my lap. I wondered if Tanner was the awkward one or maybe I was just stoned too much of the time and I was the awkward one. And if that was right, why was I stoned all the time? Then I remembered that I was coming out with my own line of weed and the reason I was stoned all the time was because I was doing research. That's a true story. I also have the Trump family to thank for my newfound love of vaping and edibles. I had to get stoned to watch the news because alcohol and outrage don't mix well—a hat on a hat.

Time speeds up as it goes by. Someone explained to me that there is a mathematical reason for this: as you age, each year becomes a smaller percentage of the life you have already lived. I'm forty-two as I write this. One year now represents a small percentage of my forty-two years (about 2.38 percent). But when I was eight, one year was a really long time; it was an eighth of my life. (This is why summer lasted about four years when you were a kid.) This may be why I now feel an urgency to know more, to do more, to be more.

Don't get me wrong—I don't believe life is too short. I

believe life is too long. It's exhausting. I don't fear dying. I want people to know that: if I die early, it's not some "tragedy"; I'd be relieved. My life has been an incredible adventure. I have $250,000 set aside for my funeral because I want everyone to have one big fucking party in my honor. I want to have a great funeral filled with dancing, little people, mushrooms—little people on mushrooms. I want it to be a celebration for all the people who love me and for all the people who are happy to see me go. (Note to self: You should probably put that money toward something more meaningful than a party for yourself—like maybe Syrian refugees or the NAACP. Just a thought.)

However, in the meantime—between now and then—this is my attempt at taking stock of how I got here, where I have been, and where it is I'm going. What exactly it is that I might bring to the table to answer the question that Viktor Frankl forced me to ask myself. Do I have the conviction to examine myself unflinchingly, to reveal the good and the bad, the ugly and the beautiful? The answer is yes. I have a lot to be embarrassed about, and I intend to advertise it.

I'm sick of my voice, of my ambition, of my entitlement. I'm sick of not knowing more, and I'm embarrassed it took me this long to recognize it. Life has been too easy. I've gotten almost everything I've ever wanted and I'm forty-two. Something smells funny.

And after all is said and done, I'd like to be cremated and have my ashes scattered over Bob Mueller's grave. Or inside it. Or his inside mine . . . or me. Or in one of Daniel Day-Lewis's clogs.

Thank you.

ROOM TEMPERATURE WATER

There was a time in my life when astrology and psychics—not to be confused with physics—fascinated me, but as a general rule, I think it's all a bunch of bullshit. Meditation seems to work for some people, while medication works for others, which explains why it's very difficult for me to sit still with my eyes closed for any length of time without Rohypnol.

I'm all for people being "spiritual," but I am leery of anyone who mentions it more than once in a single sitting, unless, of course, one is on a spiritual retreat—which I hope to God I will never be, if there even is a God. Jury's out on that one too, at least until the Rapture—an event I'm convinced will end up taking place at the Hollywood Bowl.

I believe in spirituality as a component of your lifestyle; the problem is that "spiritual people" can sometimes be giant assholes. Madonna doesn't make me want to practice Kabbalah; she makes me wonder what on earth she has on them that they are willing to let her be their most famous brand ambassador. At least Tom Cruise is a good front man for Scientology, because he *seems* nice, even though he's obviously out of his fucking tree.

I feel spiritual when I'm on mushrooms. I'm not into rocks and crystals and chakras and healers . . . I just think everyone is looking for something, and it seems like some people will settle on the first ray of sun or glimmer of hope they bump into. Los Angeles is a tricky place for vulnerable people. Hourly, you hear words like "gratitude," "universe," and "manifest," and terms like "micro–panic attack" and "artisanal deodorant." It is a place consumed with trends and fads and avocados and kale, but everything has a shelf life. There will be a point when the women and gay population of Los Angeles will turn their backs on avocados and kale—claiming they cause both cancer and erectile dysfunction—only to turn their attention toward some new colonic hydrotherapist/mystic who convinces everyone that a steady diet of fried calamari is the new anti-inflammatory food for the ages. It will quickly appear on the menu of upscale restaurants and there will be stores selling pre-packaged fresh calamari for eleven dollars a serving. It's hard to take anything or anyone seriously after a while.

· · ·

I needed to talk to someone but I was embarrassed that I needed to talk to someone. I had spent years skirting the issue of therapy based on the fact that my life was working out pretty well, minus an emotionally stable relationship with someone of the opposite sex. To anyone who would query, I would say, "I'm better off single. I don't want to be tethered to anyone. I'm not a relationship girl." My most recent favorite line was, "I'm just more high-functioning as a single person."

After all, if ninety percent of people were in relationships, then clearly I was special if I had managed to avoid one.

I was forty-two when I finally saw a real psychiatrist. I had seen doctors and therapists before, but never really with the intention of fixing anything that ran deep. I didn't have the mental equipment to articulate my pain and let someone see me for anything other than what I had become—strong. I was strong, and because of that strength, I wasn't about to sit in a doctor's office and cry. Crying for other people was fine. Crying for myself about myself was out of the question. Vulnerability in my mind was akin to carbohydrates: I wasn't willing to go there unless it was alcohol-induced.

What I didn't yet know was that when I was crying for other people, I was absolutely crying for myself.

And another thing: therapy always seemed too narcissistic—like navel-gazing. My whole entire life was about me; I've had eponymously named TV shows for the past twelve years, and a whole team of people who worked for me; and it seemed gross to sit around and spend more time talking about myself, never mind the fact that I was sick and tired of hearing the sound of my own voice. I felt like I should switch from talking to writing. Or at the very least tweeting. I just wanted to write or tweet everything, including my TV show. I looked at therapy as a horrible option; it would require listening to myself speak, rather than just speaking and having someone else edit it.

I didn't know how to ask for help—from anyone. I was surviving. My brother died when I was nine, my mother when I was thirty-one, after years of fighting cancer. My brother's death made us stronger as a family. I thought these tragedies were the reason for my tenacity. If anyone needed a strong friend, I was the one they could lean on. Give me someone else's crisis and I could fix it. I could handle anything. I was tough. It never occurred to me to wonder why I had heard so many times that people were scared of me.

"Who would ever want to be that tough?" is what one MFCC (marriage, family, and child counselor) said to me, when I'd said all of the above to him. I wasn't interested in rehashing my past—only in improving my present-day self. I said, "I just need to get better at being me."

Every therapist I saw before I reached the age of forty-two made me feel like I was running in place. I would go for a period of time and then I would eventually get bored. Often, I knew I was running circles around them. Some therapists were just not the right fit, and some of them were good but felt more like enablers than instructors, and I wanted to be taught how to be better at being a whole person. I wanted to break my pattern of ending friendships and relationships on a dime because someone did something that I found unforgivable. I would go to the mat for my friends, and sometimes for people I barely knew, and when it came time for them to return the favor or defend me, and they weren't capable of the same bullish determination I had shown them, the earth became scorched, and I wrote them off forever. Everything with me had always been black and white. Life or death. I wanted more gray. I wanted to learn how to forgive.

. . .

On an episode of my show about education, I interviewed a neuropsychiatrist and researcher named Dan Siegel, who'd written several books on developing brains, including one that focused on adolescent brains. I wanted to know when brains develop, at what age you learn the most, whether it's possible to increase your IQ, and at what age drugs and alcohol do the most damage in terms of slowing down your learning process. The last question I slipped in about three or four times throughout the conversation until I finally got the answer I wanted, which was that my brain had fully developed before any brain damage had occurred and that any extracurricular activities I was up to were just fine—at least that's what my takeaway was.

In addition to writing several books on childhood brain development and meditation, Dan lectured all over the world about mindfulness and being present, and he explained the brain to me in a very linear, non-obscure way that I could understand—with pictures.

A couple of months after the election, I had Brandon call Dan and set up an appointment.

I spent our first session talking to him about meditation, how to slow down, how to be less reactive and not end friendships every time someone hurt my feelings. I explained to him my interest in wanting to know more about the amygdala, hippocampus, and prefrontal cortex; the science of the brain would be a good non-emotional buffer while I figured out if this doctor was smarter than me.

"I like my language literal; I like logic. I can't follow anything abstract, or math, for that matter. Physics can also go fuck itself," I told him. "Also, feel free to use metaphors. I'm into those."

I kept blathering on like someone who was on a first date but was too embarrassed to admit that she was on a first date, even though she was at a restaurant with a stranger she had met online.

"I tend to lean toward my own experiences and not think outside of that perspective. It's called being selfish. It's why I'm here. To find out more about others and less about what I like. To become less self-centered, more evolved, and involved with things I know nothing about. I'm starved for a real conversation about struggle, not who the best spray-tanner in town is. I am officially dehydrated from my life."

"Okay." He nodded. "Tell me about that."

"I've decided to take this year off and throw myself into helping women and people of color get elected, because I believe we are in an emergency situation in this country, and I want to be part of the solution, not the problem. In order to do that, I feel like I have to get real about how spoiled and entitled I have become. I read somewhere that in order to be of use to others, you need to clean out your own injuries." I exhaled. "Or maybe I dreamed it. I don't know."

Dan looked at me curiously and asked me what it was exactly that I wanted to tackle, what I didn't like about myself.

"Well, I think we have to start with the fact that I can't do very simple things."

"Okay," he replied with his hands folded in his lap, legs crossed, sitting about three feet away from me. I took a deep inhale and then let it rip.

"I'd say my biggest weakness is my short fuse and my lack of ability to do any menial tasks. I've spent the last fifteen years being paid to talk for a living, so I know a lot of words and I have a lot of facial expressions and a lot of free clothes. I want to become more self-sufficient this next year. I'd like to be able to understand all these apps that everyone uses, or at least know how to download them without asking one of my assistants to do it. I'd like to know how to use the coffee machine in my kitchen; I don't drink coffee, but I'd still like to know anyway. I'd like to know how to clean up dog urine when one of my dogs pees on the rug, instead of going and sleeping in another bedroom. (I can, in fact, clean up urine when it's on a hard surface, but that rarely happens, because I believe my dogs are acutely aware of my impotence and, like typical teenagers, they like to fuck with me.) I'd like to not take scalding hot showers every day I'm home because I have no idea how to change the temperature on my own, even though it has been demonstrated for me numerous times. For the record, my shower is very complicated, but I can only take a shower when my cleaning lady is home, which means we've showered together on multiple occasions."

Dan was listening intently and seemed to be taking me

very seriously, and I wanted to disabuse him of the notion that I took myself seriously. I thought about telling him that the night before meeting him, I slept with a towel around my head because I couldn't figure out how to turn the music off in the house, but in that moment, I decided not to pile on.

"But, that's not all of me. In many moments, I have a romantic and hopeful temperament, but it usually involves being romantic and hopeful for someone else. Also, I never fill with dread. Unless, in the sense that one dreads things in the way you regret agreeing to do something you wish you hadn't said yes to, or knowing I'm about to sit down and get yelled at. I have that kind of dread. What I mean to say is that I don't have the 'doom and gloom' part. I don't get depressed. I don't have that gene. I am definitely an alarmist, and like to get myself and others fired up, but I'm not a doomsdayer. I don't think aliens are going to come out of the sky and eat us, or that I'm going to get attacked by birds, or that there's going to be a nuclear war. Well, I do worry about that, but not as an existential threat—more like it will happen, but hopefully, I'll be in Spain when it does.

"I'm a big proponent of being responsible for your own happiness," I continued, "and have always had a surfeit of dopamine to go along with it, so the only thing I really want to work on is my temper and impulse control . . . or, at the very least, behavior modification. I'm basically looking for a behaviorist. Like, for a puppy. I'd like to learn how to make my point without yelling."

Our first few sessions consisted of Dan guiding me through meditation, after which I would spend the rest of the time bitching about Donald Trump and what a piece of shit he was. I was paying someone hundreds of dollars an hour to complain about Donald Trump, which seemed like the exact right move. I would have paid him double. I had definitely paid for far worse in my life. I knew people were getting sick and tired of my anger directed toward the 2016 election and the daily horrifying cabinet appointees, and Ivanka and that schmuck Jared, and that evil witch they called a press secretary. I couldn't wrap my head around the fact that Sarah Suckabee Sanders and Ivanka Trump had no morality or sense of obligation to the very sex they inhabited—to stand up and say, *No more.* I needed someone to let me vent, privately. I needed someone to help me harness my anger into something positive.

In our third session, Dan asked me about my childhood.

"Just the usual bullshit: my parents were kind of lame, I have five brothers and sisters, one of whom died when he was twenty-two, and my mom died a few years ago—I don't really have any sense of time, so it could have been ten years ago . . . or five years, I really don't know, but I'd rather talk about *right now.* What can I do *right now?*"

He looked at me with something in his eyes that I had seen before from doctors when I mentioned that my brother had died, and that slightly annoyed me because I was paying him to talk about what *I* wanted to talk about, which was the present—not the past. It felt like pity, and that wasn't something I was interested in being on the receiving end of.

Of course I wanted to talk about my brother, but I wasn't about to admit that to a stranger.

Now, I know that I was testing him. He was earning my trust. I had to make sure I respected him, and I had to make sure he wasn't going to let me steamroll him. All I knew at the time was that I felt a responsibility, to myself and to my friends and to all the other people I loved, to keep going to my appointments with him. I didn't always feel like going—the same way I felt about meditating—but I felt that it was my duty to start doing more things that I didn't feel like doing. Something was pulling me toward him—it was as if my biological clock were telling me that I needed a psychiatrist before I wouldn't be able to reproduce anymore.

It was during our fifth or sixth session that he asked me if I had ever heard of something called the Enneagram. I hadn't. I asked him if it was a heart monitor. It's not.

The Enneagram is a psychological system based on certain ancient approaches to viewing our lives. More recently, the philosophy was adapted and popularized in the United States by a number of people as a personality test and tool for self-discovery. Dan, my therapist, and other physicians and researchers have been using variations of the Enneagram to explore the idea that there is a scientifically recognized brain-based personality pattern that develops and manifests over the course of our lives. Dan applies something called a PDP model, which stands for patterns of developmental pathways. Basically, this method suggests that most people are born with a tendency toward one of three default zones based on how you contend with the separation that occurs when you leave the womb, where you are safe and warm and nourished for nine months, and are then catapulted into a hospital room with harsh fluorescent lights shining on you (if you're lucky), where you are greeted with a smack on the ass and you have to cry every time you want to eat or are in pain, because suddenly that's the only way to communicate your needs. Or something like that. Anyway, Dan says how you navigate this transition from the inner peace of the womb to the struggles of the world outside of it is an important factor in determining your personality.

I gave him a skeptical look. When he asked me what I was thinking, I told him that this sounded very LA.

"What do you mean?" he asked earnestly.

"You know . . . I mean, are people really holding on to their births all these years later? I just find that a little hard to believe. Now people are going to be pissed about being born? It's a little much, no?"

He cocked his head to the side, and I didn't know if it was meant to challenge me, or if he was sincerely confused by my Los Angeles reference.

"I just have a hard time comprehending why rehashing the past repeatedly, time and time again, is beneficial to people who just need to get up and move the fuck on. Get over it. There are people being blown out of their homes in Syria. We have a president who is rolling back women's rights, and innocent black men are getting shot and killed by police officers every day. Get out of your own asshole, and look around."

The irony that I was sitting in a psychiatrist's office complaining about people who sit in a psychiatrist's office was not lost on either of us. We locked eyes with an intense stare because what I had admitted was more profound than anything I was blabbering on about; I had sought out the help of a professional because I knew, on a cellular level, that I wouldn't be able to help anyone in a real, meaningful way until I was able to sit with myself—a place I believed I was too smart to ever have to go to.

"Okay, that's fair," he said, nodding, understanding where I was coming from. "Just so you know, from my professional experience, I have seen how it has helped a lot of people to understand themselves and the people they love in a deeper way. But we don't have to talk about it. It's totally up to you."

I told him what my father told me about taking one piece of information away from any conversation and that one of my desires was to become more open-minded, as long as I was learning something, and if this was something he believed in, I was willing to hear him out.

"Your father sounds like a smart guy," Dan said.

"Well, let's not get carried away. I mean, he was and is smart, but he's also a con man who cheated, lied, and probably stole from people. He is the epitome of a used-car dealer."

"In what way?"

"He actually was a used-car dealer."

"Ah, okay."

"But please go on, because I'm here to become less judgmental, and more patient, and if I really lose interest in this subject matter, I'll start rolling my eyes, which is also something I'd like to do less frequently."

He went on to tell me that this default zone is the place you revert to when you feel uncomfortable, or nervous, or when things don't turn out the way they were supposed to.

When you are born into this world, you experience one of the three reactions, which sets up your disposition in life. In the Enneagram model, the reactions are located in the head, heart, and gut. Dan and his fellow researchers developed their own model, translating those three areas of the body to emotional states: fear (head), sadness (heart), and anger (gut).

"I'm anger."

"Okay."

"I'm fucking angry. I just don't understand how this man could get elected."

Dan told me to just sit with that feeling and not talk.

What I grew to learn was that Dan didn't want me to talk around my anger and pretend it was all about Donald Trump. What Donald Trump represented to me were things being out of control, and when things became unhinged, I became angry because that was my default zone. I realize that many people may think of me as someone who is completely out of control myself, and they're not wrong. I am out of control, but within boundaries that no one knows about except me. I thrive in organized chaos. It keeps my juices flowing and it keeps me paying attention and on my tippy-toes.

Once the silence had gone on for what seemed to me like an unreasonable amount of time (less than a minute), I needed to break it.

"Anger makes sense," I admitted. "All I ever wanted was financial freedom and independence and now I have it, but I'm stuck. I'm stuck with what to do next, because the whole world is upside down. Until I read Rebecca Solnit and James Baldwin and Ta-Nehisi Coates I had no idea how many women are beaten and raped every second in this world or what it means to grow up as a black person, or any person of color, in this country we call 'the land of the free and the home of the brave.' What is wrong with me? How could I be so self-absorbed?"

I was saying things out loud I hadn't said out loud to anyone before.

"I've spent the last fifteen years of my success believing that I picked myself up by my bootstraps and worked my ass off to get where I was. It never occurred to me that I have had an advantage just by being white. That I've never *not* argued with a police officer when being pulled over for a ticket, while for black people getting pulled over is a life-or-death situation. I've been so consumed with my own success and my own personal life that I haven't spent enough time thinking about people outside my lane and what their struggles are. I have shame for my entitlement and for not learning all of this sooner. I feel great shame and outrage. I'm embarrassed for our entire race, but I'm really mostly embarrassed for myself."

By the time I was done with this little diatribe, my eyes were starting to water. I needed to pivot and change topics before the lip-quivering kicked in. It would be mortifying to lose my composure in front of a stranger. I was not going to let myself cry.

"I come on strong."

"To whom?"

"To anyone who I think needs me."

"Tell me more about that."

"I want to fix people. If someone doesn't have friends, I'll introduce them to people. If someone needs money, I'll give them money. If someone is hurt and is going through a breakup in Germany, I will fly to Germany to be with them. They don't really even have to be a close friend. I'd do that for a stranger. I have a boundary issue, I think. Why do I do these things unless I am making up for some other terrible quality that I'm trying to camouflage? It's too much. I always go too far. I'm like a calf that needs to be faked out with an electric fence inside a bigger electric fence, like a Russian nesting doll. I have to be tricked to stay inbounds. Like an animal. I hate boundaries."

Dan looked at me with concern, but it was concern that I needed. I needed someone who didn't know me to be concerned for me, and it seemed like a more straightforward transaction to pay someone to do it.

"Okay, so, back to the Enneagram," I said. "So, how you enter this world determines your natural disposition for the rest of your life? Is this astrology-adjacent?"

"I don't view it as that, no. But if you are hesitant about diving in further, then we don't have to discuss it at all."

"You have a medical degree, right?"

"I do." He nodded, smiling. "I've also trained as a researcher, so a lot of the research I've done on the Enneagram with other scientists and other researchers is something I'm very familiar with. If I didn't think it held any merit, I wouldn't be writing about it or talking about it."

Okay, calm down, big guy is what I wanted to say, but I felt at that point he had gotten a full dose of my cynicism, and the truth was that I *did* want to hear more.

"Obviously, there are other factors, such as nature and nurture, along with all of the events that happen throughout your early childhood and throughout your life that will shape who you become as a person," he said. "But that anger, sadness, or fear will remain deep in your subconscious, and will dictate how you react to things in your life that don't go as planned."

Dan asked me about my parents' marriage, and I told him it was functionally dysfunctional. That my parents were hard to take seriously as role models, but that my aversion to being married wasn't about my parents' marriage. It was about marriage in general; it seemed outdated.

"I consider remaining unmarried a victory," I told him. "If I had married either of the men I'd thought about marrying, I would be divorced . . . therefore ending up as just another statistic. Conversely, remaining married to the same person your entire life seems not only boring, but also like becoming just another statistic. It feels like marriage goes hand in hand with, well . . . running errands, or baking."

"You don't run errands?" he asked, slightly confused.

"I try not to."

I worked hard to maintain eye contact with him when I took breaks from rambling so that he would understand I was serious, even if some of the things I said sounded ridiculous. I was serious about getting help for my ridiculousness.

"Sorry, I know you're married, and it's not an insult," I told him. "I just prefer to not do what everyone else is doing. I like to be in the minority."

"No offense taken," he assured me, smiling slightly.

"I think I'm more cut out for short flings, or long-distance relationships, casual encounters. I don't think I have what it takes to remain interested in someone long term. The word 'marriage' has always felt to me like the end of fun."

"Okay," he said, leaning his head to one side.

"I don't like constraints or restrictions of any kind. I don't like feeling boxed in. A one-on-one beach holiday with someone of the opposite sex is something I'd like to avoid at all costs. I'd rather be alone."

At this point in my life, I didn't know if anything I was saying was true or if I had manufactured all these thoughts to protect myself—I'm assuming it's the latter, but the truth of the matter is when it comes to men, I haven't been that impressed with my choices.

He asked me why I thought marriage represented the end of fun.

"I get bored easily, and I also go at things in a wildly immature way."

"How so?"

"Like a little girl. Everything has to be the most, or the best, or dangerous, or a risk. I take everything too far. I don't know how to just be still, unless I'm lying in bed binge-watching *Peaky Blinders* or if I'm at a long, leisurely lunch, anywhere pleasant in this world. Then I can sit for hours, but that scenario involves Aperol spritzes and other people who feel as passionately as I do about Aperol spritzes. This is why I can't meditate."

"Because of Aperol spritzes?"

"Because I like extremes. I think I'm an extremist."

"Tell me about that."

"It's the 'everything is a possibility' phase that I live for.

I don't ever want another person making the decisions about where I go or what I do, or to be sent down a particular runway I haven't approved. I want to change runways all the time, and I don't like answering to others. I don't like feeling trapped, or having to get approval to go on a trip from anyone. I want to do what I want to do when I want to do it. I'm completely fucking spoiled."

"Okay, talk more about that," he said.

"I feel like I'm always running a million miles an hour, and that I've covered a lot of ground, and I like that my life is so full. I've had so many adventures, but there are never enough. There's too much to see, too many books I haven't read, and too many people that need help. I do feel grateful. When I stop being grateful for something, I usually end it. I stopped doing stand-up because I burned myself out. I did too many shows and too much traveling and wrote too many books in a row to be grateful. It became rote. I was becoming devoid of the joy one should have when walking out to a crowd of thousands of people. I grew impatient and irritable, and I felt icky having those thoughts in front of people who had paid money to come see me, all the while dying for it to be over so I could just hang out with whoever was on the road with me. I didn't enjoy being on the stage as much as I enjoyed walking off it. I liked the sense of accomplishment—and all the great luxurious things that came with it—but once I realized my heart wasn't in it, I felt like I was ripping people off, and I was done."

"What does it feel like to you when you are not running around making yourself busy?" he asked me, leaning forward in his chair, putting both hands on his knees.

"I have no idea, because I've never done that. This is what I do with everything. I burn the candle at both ends, and then I grow bored."

"Do you think that you're running from something?"

"I don't know, because that's how I've always gone through life," I told him. "I get sick of people, places, jobs, things. I'm always looking for newness. Something fresh, someone new, a stranger, the unknown."

I told him that when I was a kid I was so hungry to grow up and become famous and successful that my entire twenties and half of my thirties were spent in a cycle of feeding that hunger and then looking for something else. I had now reached the burnout phase with my talk show. I was sick of all the things that went along with doing a talk show. The editing, the talent booking, the constant micromanaging, and having to watch myself on camera over and over again.

I was over it.

Dan asked me about children, and I repeated what I tell everyone who asks. "I've never had the urge. It wouldn't be a good use of my time."

I asked him to tell me more about fear and sadness. I wanted to make sure I could rule those two things out.

He told me that people whose default is fear tend to second-guess everything they do. They tend to be indecisive, and many end up leading very safe lives. They are not interested in risk or adventure—they are interested in sameness and security. They are people who typically do not switch careers midlife or go skydiving or take great risks. They are also conflict-averse.

"Yeah, no," I said. "That's not me. I'm into conflict."

The people who live in sadness tend to be depressives

and can struggle with that their entire lives. They typically have huge amounts of empathy for others. These people also tend to love animals more than the average person loves animals. They are sensitive to others and are typically great listeners, but again, they can also have serious issues with depression.

"Yeah, I'm anger."

"Okay, so you're anger. Let's start there."

He explained that the Enneagram system starts by identifying which of the three states of mind you are most closely aligned with and then broadens into a total of nine different personality types.

"I can describe each type to you and we can try to figure out which one you are, which will help you understand why you do some of the things you do, and what areas you can strengthen—that's called your 'growth edge.'"

Dan went through each of the nine personality types and told me to think of them like spokes on a wheel, which was also his analogy to meditation: spokes on a wheel. Start with your breath, then your hearing, your sight, and then keep going around the wheel to your internal organs and then your external body parts. I appreciated this because it was another visual aid—something I've learned over the years is the most effective way for me to digest a concept I'm unfamiliar with. Everything was all about spokes on a wheel. The Wheel of Awareness is what he calls it. Dan liked wheels, and my guess is that in a past life he drove a wagon—on wheels.

The Enneagram captured my interest because I respected the person who was telling me about it. When going through the nine different personality types, you'll find that some include characteristics you recognize in yourself, but there are usually one or two traits that stand out as definitely not part of your personality. Ultimately, the number that describes you the most accurately is the one in which all the traits apply to you. There are tests you can take online to find your number—some more extensive than others—but it is ultimately about reading each number's strengths and weaknesses, and being honest with yourself, about yourself.

Dan also explained that, typically, people feel drawn to two numbers at first. Then you revisit those two numbers, paying attention to the weaknesses of each. That's when you are usually able to discern which number more aptly describes you, and lock into one of the numbers, which is what happened to me.

When we got to number seven, I started to hear things that sounded like me.

7

THE ENTHUSIAST

Enneagram Type Seven

The Busy, Variety-Seeking Type:
Spontaneous, Versatile, Acquisitive, and Scattered

TYPE SEVEN IN BRIEF

Sevens are extroverted, optimistic, versatile, and spontaneous. Playful, high-spirited, and practical, they can also misapply their many talents, becoming over-extended, scattered, and undisciplined. They constantly seek new and exciting experiences, but can become distracted and exhausted by staying on the go. They typically have problems with impatience and impulsiveness. *At their best:* they focus their talents on worthwhile goals, becoming appreciative, joyous, and satisfied.

Basic Fear: Of being deprived and in pain

Basic Desire: To be satisfied and content—to have their needs fulfilled

Key Motivations: Want to maintain their freedom and happiness, to avoid missing out on worthwhile experiences, to keep themselves excited and occupied, to avoid and discharge pain.

Type Seven sounded a lot like me, until I heard the description of Type Eight, and realized that I'm not positive enough to be a seven; I'm more of a half-glass-period person. I don't see a glass as half empty or half full—it's just half; it could go either way.

8
THE CHALLENGER
Enneagram Type Eight
The Powerful, Dominating Type:
Self-Confident, Decisive, Willful, and Confrontational

TYPE EIGHT IN BRIEF
Eights are self-confident, strong, and assertive. Protective, resourceful, straight-talking, and decisive, but can also be egocentric and domineering. Eights feel they must control their environment, especially people, sometimes becoming confrontational and intimidating. Eights typically have problems with their tempers and with allowing themselves to be vulnerable. *At their best:* self-mastering, they use their strength to improve others' lives, becoming heroic, magnanimous, and inspiring.

Basic Fear: Of being harmed or controlled by others

Basic Desire: To protect themselves (to be in control of their own life and destiny)

Key Motivations: Want to be self-reliant, to prove their strength and resist weakness, to be important in their world, to dominate the environment, and to stay in control of their situation.

"I'm an eight."

"Okay, you're an eight, then."

"Do you think I'm an eight?"

"That's the thing about the Enneagram," he said. "You can't assess someone else. Each person has to assess themselves."

"That's what I do," I told Dan. "I'm a fixer. I charge in and clean up messes. Everyone's except my own. What are the bad qualities about being an eight?"

He reassured me that there were no bad numbers, and I reassured him that I wasn't sensitive enough to care if some numbers were bad or good, but that if we were going to work on my weaknesses, we needed to get real.

Dan told me about a conference he attended where he sat alone with groups of only sevens or groups of only eights and had asked them all what the best-kept secret of being that number was—the one thing that each number needed to work on the most.

"And?"

"All the eights said that their hidden secret is that eights lack empathy," Dan said.

Lack of empathy. Huh.

"Like a Republican?"

I had to think about the difference between empathy and sympathy. I can be too sympathetic to people. I'm a sucker for a sob story and I will lavish sympathy on any stranger who needs a hand. But empathy? I had to talk that through with him.

"Empathy and sympathy? What's the distinction, again?"

"Sympathy is feeling bad for someone or for their situation. Sympathy is more like pity. Empathy is imagining what it's like to be in that person's shoes. Thinking about what it feels like to be another person and the understanding that their experiences and outlooks may have been unlike your own. Actually, thinking about what it's like to *be* them."

Dan asked me about those instances when I show up for people I care about and if, while I'm doing it, I think about what it feels like to be in that person's predicament.

The answer was no.

I went to their bedside, or doorstep, or lay in bed with any of my friends who needed a friend in order to do one thing: fix the situation.

To show up repeatedly, time and time again. Whenever that happens, my sympathy is in full gear, but rarely if ever do I consider what it's like to be that person in that moment. I want to wrap their injury and patch them up. I never stop showing up, but I don't put myself in their shoes. Often we think we are showing up for someone, when really all we're doing is showing everyone how great we are at showing up.

Lack of empathy.

That hit me over the head.

I have no empathy. Yes! That's right! Like how I feel about people who like room temperature water. Some people don't care about the temperature of their drink or the quality of ice. I don't understand those people. Like, when flight attendants hand out room temperature Dasani water, I want to throw it out the airplane window. I've always looked sideways at this community of humans who are okay with room temperature water, or—God forbid—prefer it. Or people who like pineapple on their pizza or, for that matter, any other hot food with pineapple on it.

Rosemary annoys the shit out of me too, but everyone else seems to fucking love it. Then again, I love cilantro, and people can have a visceral reaction to that, and I don't get that at all. How could anyone hate cilantro? It feels like I just need to meet more people who hate rosemary as much as I do. But mostly everything and everyone, at some point, ends up annoying me. And now I know why. I'm not thinking about them. I have gone through life failing to understand why people have different reactions to things than I do.

Lack of empathy made total sense. I never understand why everyone doesn't just do what I would do: Get up and trudge on. Power through. So: I have sympathy, but not empathy. I also have zero sentimentality. It's almost like I'm allergic to it—like, when people talk about missing an old car or a home they've sold . . . I just want to tell them to please move on to the next topic, *quickly*. I can't relate at all.

I was on board with being an Eight who lacked empathy. Doorways in my brain were opening.

I realize the hypocrisy of me espousing a philosophy that used a number to describe my personality, for fuck's sake, but I do feel passionately about takeaways, especially honest ones, and this was the first time a professional had told me something about myself that was negative. I had a takeaway. No empathy was huge. That was something tangible that I could learn from—a growth edge. I didn't care how hokey this sounded; the bottom line was that I had more information. Finding out what my weaknesses were opened the floodgates. Even if it's a theory or a little astrology- or numerology-adjacent, if it rings true with you, then it is true to you, and that's really all anyone needs in order to forge ahead and improve themselves. I needed to get past a roadblock, and understanding I had no empathy was a big first step.

· · ·

METANOIA

Metanoia.

Noun.

A profound transformation in one's outlook.

USAGE: "You'll need to rethink everything. Here you'll need to resort to old-style metanoia, to radical rethinking and alteration."

—Alois Brandstetter, *The Abbey* (Ariadne Press, 1998)

Finding out I lacked empathy was my metanoia.

I spent the next few weeks recalling one instance after another where I now recognized my lack of empathy.

I had been in London with one of my best friends, who happens to be a gay man. We went to see the movie *Call Me by Your Name*. Five minutes in, I leaned over, irritated, and asked, "Is this a gay love story?"

"Yes," he hissed, incredulously. I hadn't known what the movie was about going in, and I was taken by surprise.

"Oh, my God. You're so selfish," I whispered loudly,

while I shoveled popcorn down my throat. The ludicrousness of my comment hit us both at the same time, and we started laughing so disruptively, we had to remove ourselves ten minutes into the movie.

Gay people have had to sit through straight people's stories since the beginning of time. *Had I ever thought about that?* Nope. Never occurred to me.

Lack of empathy was everywhere I went. This was an exciting development.

. . .

I had been seeing Dan for just over a month—about two times a week—and I felt like I was making substantial progress in terms of not being reactive. I was now thinking about things before saying them, which prior to me seeing this doctor I had never even contemplated as a possible way to behave. I was in a particularly good mood that day when I walked into his office, excited to tell him that I was getting somewhere with my behavior, and that I actually enjoyed the three-minute meditation I had done that morning—that I might even be ready to bump it up to five minutes.

When I got to his office and sat down, Dan handed me an orange.

"I felt like you might want an orange today. I picked it from my tree."

This was the moment I became undone.

In that moment, I fell apart at the proverbial seams.

Shoulders down, head bowed.

I sat and cried and shook and let my shoulders feel sorry for themselves and my heart ached and I moaned, loudly—

like a wounded wolf. One with an injury that had scabbed over many times but had never properly healed. I had a deep infection.

My crying was acute, hysterical. It was the kind of guttural pain that could land you in the hospital. I cried, and cried, and cried, all while peeling my orange, with Dan sitting there looking at me like he had expected this all along. He handed me a box of tissues, which I used to clean up the juice that was squirting everywhere because, apparently, peeling an orange was another simple task that I had somehow magically forgotten how to do, and had instead been stabbing it with my fingernails.

I wanted to charge past my tears, to stop myself from crying in front of him—or anyone, for that matter—but he left me with no other avenues. I had no choice but to give in and let it rip and let him watch me crumble. Foam-at-the-mouth, snot-out-of-the-nose kind of crying. Nothing I'd ever want another person to see me do. All while still trying to maintain some sort of dignity by continuing to eat my orange, which was a mess with the makeshift plate I had made out of the tissues, and when I felt more tears coming my way, I gave up the life raft. I put the tissues and the half-molested orange in my lap and looked at his trustworthy, smarter-than-me eyes and saw in them what I had been longing for all along—*pity*. After thirty years of bottling up the deepest injury of my life, I was ready for someone to feel sorry for me.

. . .

We had met in a different room that day. Dan's regular office was being used by someone else, so he warned me at our last appointment that we would have to meet in his other office, which we hadn't done before. I remember thinking, *What kind of a basket case does he think I am that he has to warn me about sitting in a different office?*

I don't know if it was the change of scenery, or if it was because the light was different, or that we were sitting at a table rather than in our regular two chairs—or if it was that simple act of kindness of him giving me an orange he had picked from his tree that elicited such a primal reaction inside me.

When I was finally able to collect myself, I said, "There's nothing I hate more than room temperature fruit, and I almost never eat carbs, but I'm going to eat this orange, and thank you for bringing it to me."

"You're welcome."

Then I exhaled for about ten minutes straight—putting myself back together—and when I was finally able to breathe normally again, he asked me what I was feeling.

"Anger," I sobbed. "I'm so angry, and I'm so tired."

"I bet," he said. "I bet you are."

"I need to tell you about the day my brother died, and what happened to my family."

DEATH
VALLEY

My brother was the first man I ever slept with. The night I came home from the hospital, my mom said that Chet, who was thirteen at the time, asked if he could sleep with me, to which my mom . . . agreed? Over the years, he told the story of not being able to sleep that whole night for fear of rolling over and crushing me. The better question—I've always thought—was why either of my parents allowed a thirteen-year-old boy to sleep with a two-day-old baby. That should give you some insight into how interested my parents were in raising children or, for that matter, using protection. They had six children, and it's a miracle any of us are still breathing.

. . .

I heard him taking two steps at a time up to my mom's room, so I ducked my head under the covers, where I was snuggling with my mother in our usual spot. My mom was the definition of a snuggler, and she always had some form of chocolate close by. A Snickers, or an Almond Joy, or a brownie wrapped in cellophane. Lying in bed with her was like sleeping with cotton candy.

"Where is *she?*" Chet asked, menacingly, when he bombed through the bedroom door, smelling like the woods. My brother always smelled like a bonfire. He smelled like the beach and the woods all at the same time. He smelled like home.

"She's not *heeere,*" my mom sang in the singsong, flirty way she spoke when she was being playful, which was a large percentage of the time.

"I don't believe you," he told her and then pinpointed exactly where my feet were, grabbed them, and dragged me out of the bed, until he was holding me upside down by my ankles, with my head an inch above the floor. I used my arms to climb up his legs, and then he spun me around until I was over his shoulders.

"Be careful, Chet," my mom scolded my brother, which was silly because a) she knew I loved this, and b) my mother telling any of us to be careful didn't even go in one ear and out the other—it just turned around and went right back into her mouth.

"What's for dinner?" he asked me, as we bounded down the steps to the kitchen.

It was after ten P.M., and whenever Chet came home from work that late, he wanted cereal. When I was nine years old, preparing cereal felt culinary and also made me feel like I was running a household, which no one else in my family seemed to be doing at that point. I fancied myself a homemaker, taking care of my brood.

Being the youngest of six doesn't beg a lot of service from your siblings; no one ever asked me for anything—but Chet did. I loved making him cereal when he came home late. I could make any kind of cereal. I knew the right milk-to-cereal ratio he preferred, so I'd fold a paper towel into a napkin (my parents had either never heard about napkins or they were able to buy paper towels cheaper and in bulk), and place a cereal spoon beside the bowl because, unlike anyone else in our family, I knew the difference between a cereal spoon and a teaspoon. (To this day, I always prefer a cereal spoon, even when I'm drinking tea.) Then we'd sit at the kitchen table and talk about our day—like a couple.

My brother Chet was the oldest, then twenty-two, and I was the youngest. I was his little plaything. I knew that the more outrageous I was, the more he would howl, and I loved the feeling of making him howl, with his head thrown back, laughing. Chet was tall and skinny—but strong enough to throw me over his shoulders. I always braced myself when I saw him charge through a room, headed in my direction, with his eyes dancing. I'd try to duck or run, but would freeze in the end, covering my head in my hands, kicking and screaming, only to be thrown up over his shoulders and taken somewhere that I pretended I didn't want to go. I wanted to go everywhere with him. He could build a shed, he could sail a boat, and he could fix a car—three things my father could never do, but pretended to do frequently.

I would watch Chet and my father in the garage, while Chet would mimic closing the hood of the car on my father's head or dance around making funny faces at me while my father asked him for some tool that he thought would aid in restarting the engine of whatever outdated jalopy he had his head under. Even as a kid, that felt so silly to watch; sitting there, I was embarrassed for my own father, pretending he could do things that he couldn't. Chet was an actual engineer, so he understood mechanics, and when my father would eventually throw his hands up, having exhausted all possibilities (known to him), Chet would step in and actually fix the car. Chet was a man the day he was born. My dad seemed like a boy who got big.

They call it a *macher* in Yiddish. All talk, very little action. My father always made grand sweeping hand gestures when he spoke, which is one of the various bad habits I picked up from him. My brother never moved his hands when he spoke. He didn't have to.

Most nights, I would fall asleep on the couch in Chet's room—or I'd pretend to fall asleep, because that's how I got him to carry me. He'd pick me up off the couch in the same way you'd pick up a handicapped person, and that's when I felt the warmest feeling in the world—like I was being looked after. I knew in those steps to my room that I was loved. That the man I loved the most loved me right back.

Having an older brother is a lot like a crush—in fact, it is a crush. You have someone you love and adore, who never loses his temper with you, who is always looking out for you and looking after you, and that becomes your definition of what love means.

Maybe I've canonized my brother into something much more than he was. Did his smile linger a little longer at me in my memories? Perhaps. But maybe he smiled even more than I'm giving him credit for. Maybe he was even *more* than I remember. But this is my memory, the one that has been stuck in my head for over thirty years . . . collecting dust.

One August, we were coming back from Martha's Vineyard at the end of our summer—a five-hour car ride from Woods Hole, Massachusetts, to Livingston, New Jersey. Chet knew how much I loved the cold air, so he wrapped me up in blankets and rolled down the windows, and we drove like that the whole way home, listening to Neil Young. When I'd open my eyes a crack to make sure he wasn't too cold, he'd shiver dramatically in his flannel shirt and say, "God, this is miserable," with a huge smirk on his face—or maybe smirk isn't the right word. It was less than a smile and more than a smirk. It was a grin. Chet always had that grin.

When we finally pulled into our driveway late that night, I wasn't asleep, but I pretended to be. He carried me up the stairs to my room, singing some silly commercial about a ferryboat in Falmouth, Massachusetts, that was always on the radio. *Sail away to Falmouth, / Sail away on the Island Queen* . . . Then he tucked me in bed—wide-awake, with my eyes closed—and turned the fan that was sitting on my nightstand to high. He was the only person in my family who understood that I was born going through menopause, and that whenever I ate soup, I had to take my top off. He always made me feel like precious cargo.

. . .

"Why do you want to go hiking? For what?" I wanted to know, through bites of cereal. "Is it because you have a *girlfriend*?"

"*No*, it's not because I have a *girlfriend*." My brother crinkled his nose a lot when he was teasing me, and then I'd crinkle my nose back—like we were on the show *Bewitched*, minus the sound effects.

He told me that he was going to California to rent a car and then drive from there to the Grand Canyon and Zion Canyon, and then on to hike the Grand Tetons.

"You're going to be on the Vineyard, anyway. You won't even be here," he said through bites of my signature dish of Raisin Bran and sliced bananas.

"Why do you have to go?" I asked him. "Why don't you just come to the Vineyard with us? I don't want to drive with Mom to the Vineyard." My mom drove very slowly, hated having the windows open on a freeway, and listened to Dr. Laura Schlessinger.

"I want to drive with you," I whined.

I was too young to think about anyone else's interests but my own. Too young to think that maybe he deserved a fucking vacation after graduating from college and looking after our whole family his entire life. Too young to consider what it must have been like to be him and the sense of responsibility he must have felt to all of us—including my parents. Too young to know that people take vacations without their families.

"It's only two weeks. I'll be back before you know it, and then I'll come straight to the Vineyard when I'm back. You won't even know I'm gone. By the end of the summer, you'll be wishing I had stayed on vacation because I am going to make sure that every single day we go sailing, you are going to end up in the bay with Bruce."

I flicked a banana slice off my spoon in his direction.

Bruce was the mechanical shark from the movie *Jaws*. Parts of *Jaws* were filmed in Katama Bay in front of our house on Martha's Vineyard the year I was born. My brothers and sisters believed he still lived in the bay—even though filming had concluded nine years prior.

Sailing with Chet was the best adventure ever. He had a little Sunfish sailboat and would take some of us, or all of us, out on the bay in front of our house, and almost every single time, at some point—you'd never know exactly when—he'd suddenly tip the boat over, and whoever was in the boat ended up in the water screaming. Laughter combined with the terror of bumping into the remains of Bruce.

Then he would tip the boat back on its right side, get himself up, and come lift me out of the water. Then he'd pin me down on the boat and accuse me of tipping over the boat. For some reason, the silliness of this made me laugh even harder, and all my siblings knew that if I was laughing hard, peeing in my pants was right around the corner. That's when he'd throw me back into the water again. Rinse, cycle, repeat. The thrill was real every time. Danger, but with the cushion of safety. I can still smell the orange life jackets he made us wear, and not because they smelled like urine. They smelled like my brother—salt and wood and beach and home.

. . .

"I need a little vacation, Chels. Do you really think I'd leave you with these people?" His nose was crinkling again, and I made a sad face and tried not to cry. My brother was like a father to me, but far less embarrassing. He was handsome and he wasn't obese. My father wasn't obese at this point in our lives, but all the signs were pointing in that direction.

My dad was in charge of everything. He ran the show and he was the person who said no to things. My mom said yes to everything. Candy at any time during the day, she didn't care whether or not you cleaned your room, or what time you went to bed, or if you brushed your teeth—or hair, for that matter. I could have gone to school pantsless if I wanted to—it's actually surprising I didn't.

My mom was the one you always wanted to be home. She was fine with whichever way the wind blew. I once walked into our summer house on a rainy day with a six-pack of Heineken that my friend and I stole from her parents' fridge. "We're going to try beer," I told my mom, who just rolled her eyes, and went back to crocheting my father a sweater. I was ten.

My dad was the problem. He was the one we were all scared of. If any of our brothers or sisters wanted anything, it was up to Chet or me to ask. Chet was the oldest, and I was the youngest. We were bookends.

. . .

It was around nine P.M. when my sister Simone and I walked into our house on the Vineyard, and as soon as we did, my mother was at the top of the stairs with a face I'd never seen before. She looked distorted. Her face was blotchy and she was leaning on the banister, clutching herself. It looked like she had been attacked.

Simone took what was left of our ice cream cones and headed to the kitchen to toss them into the trash. I stood frozen, looking at my mother, who wasn't talking, and I was wondering if there was an intruder in the house. And if so, were we supposed to run out of the house to get the police and leave her there? *No, we can't do that. Was he still in the house? What was happening? Why wasn't anyone saying anything?* Seconds felt like minutes.

Simone came back from the kitchen to the bottom of the stairwell, where I was standing, still frozen, and looked at me with dread in her eyes, and then looked up at my mother's distorted face.

"Your brother's dead."

My mom didn't specify which brother, because she didn't have to. Simone and I both knew it was Chet. He had gone on a trip and didn't stay with the family, and now he was gone forever.

Just like that.

You don't believe these moments when they happen. You believe they have the wrong guy—that it was his friend, it wasn't him. Your brain is moving so fast thinking of all the things that have changed in just the blink of an eye—what it all means. *It means we are five. Not six anymore.* It meant our family was broken.

There are only five of us now. That's not the right number.

We need six. Six is our number. We are a team. Now I have a dead brother? What do you mean, "dead"? Is that final?

I ran into the bedroom at the bottom of the stairs and threw myself onto the bed and cried and screamed and wailed in agony. Death is agony. There is simply no other way to describe it. It is getting the wind knocked out of you over and over again, and just when you think you have enough strength to take a deep breath, it knocks you down again. There is no break from the pain. It is arduous, un-yielding.

I remember thinking, *This is what you're supposed to do now: Jump onto the bed and bury your face in your tears. Just pretend you're acting. Do what they do on soap operas.*

I didn't think about my mother or my father or my brothers or my sisters. All I could think about was what he said to me—that he lied to me. My brother left me with the very people he said he wouldn't. My bookend was gone, and now things were really out of control.

No, no, no. This isn't happening. It isn't him. It can't be. He's too strong to die. They're going to find his body and find out it's someone else's brother. I got down on my knees and prayed for someone else's brother to be dead.

· · ·

"You have to get up. We have to help Mom. You need to come upstairs and be with Mom." It was Simone. Simone was the oldest girl and Chet was the oldest boy. She had just lost her partner too. That never occurred to me then.

I sat on the bed with my mom as she recounted my fa-ther's phone call from New Jersey. I remember sitting there, wondering if this was what she was going to look like from now on—a foreigner.

She said when my dad called to tell her, she only heard moaning on the other side of the phone. The police had come to my father's door, and somehow knowing he had a heart condition—he'd had a heart attack a year earlier—they had sat him down before they told him. He couldn't talk when he called my mom. He just kept moaning into the phone until the police took the phone and told my mother what had happened.

Years later, my sister Shoshanna was telling someone the story of how she found out Chet had died, and it was similar to mine.

"You weren't there," I told her. "You weren't with us."

"Of course I was there, Chelsea. We were all there together. I came home from babysitting, and you and Simone were upstairs with Mom. Simone went outside while Mom told me because, I guess, she couldn't bear to hear the news twice."

I had no recollection of Shana being there that night. I only remember Simone taking me out for ice cream at the Dairy Queen in Edgartown, and bumping into some of her friends at the gas station, and they asked about Chet.

"He's in Wyoming, hiking. He'll be back next week."

The thing I remember most vividly is the ice cream and Simone knowing to throw it away when she saw my mother's grief-stricken face. She knew before my mother said a word to throw the ice cream away. I remember wanting to ask her why we needed to throw away perfectly good ice cream, but I knew enough not to.

I remember our neighbor coming over with a bottle of red wine, which I remember thinking was inappropriate, because we weren't celebrating. I remember wondering why all of the sudden we liked our neighbor when all we'd done was talk about what a pain in the ass she was. I didn't understand why she was at our house, or why my mother who almost never drank alcohol was drinking red wine.

I remember waking up in the morning and thinking that all deaths should happen in the daylight. All bad news should come in the morning. That way, you have the whole day to get used to your new reality, so that the first daylight you see after death doesn't feel like a plane nosediving into the ocean with the damage becoming worse the deeper into the sea you go. In death, the aftermath is worse than the crash.

My mom packed up our family van, and we got on the very first ferry off the island to Woods Hole and drove the five hours back to New Jersey. No one spoke.

. . .

My father and my brother Roy walked out the front door when we pulled into our driveway. Chet's car was parked on the bottom left-hand side. Roy and my dad were both crying and walking toward us like zombies, with their arms open. I had never seen my father cry before, and I didn't like it. It was sunny out, which made no sense to me. Birds were chirping. The weather was not commensurate with death.

I wanted everyone to go inside. *Not on the lawn. Not like this in front of all the neighbors.*

I bypassed all the hugging and went inside to look for Chet. If his car was in the driveway, it meant that he was home. *I bet nobody even looked in his room.* I walked into his room and could smell him. I looked in his closet and I smelled his flannel shirts. Then I called out his name, but it was like one of those dreams where no sound comes out. *This can't be happening. This can't happen. Our family can't take a hit like this.*

I remember thinking there was no way my parents had budgeted for a funeral. The domino effect of Chet going off and letting himself die was going to be brutal.

How could he have let this happen?

Then there were the optics. Now everyone would know for sure our family was broken, because now our family really *was* broken. We were already skating on thin ice because my parents were known to be less than traditional and a little bit too lackadaisical. No other adults or parents seemed to take an interest in getting to know either of my parents, nor did any clear-thinking adult allow their children to spend time at our house, with such a lack of supervision. Now we had a dead brother because my parents let their son go hiking in the Grand Tetons and he had never hiked a mountain like that before. They were unfit, and now there was proof.

There were people in and out of our house all week. We sat shivah, which, for those of you who aren't familiar with Jewish customs, is a week of mourning for the loss of a loved one—with a lot of deli meat.

People came over with deli platters and all sorts of food—smoked fish, cakes, pies, cookies—everything seemed so unappealing. There was a never-ending supply of corned beef and hot pastrami. Your thoughts become so miscellaneous. I remember looking at all these people I didn't know who were in our house and trying to figure out the difference between corned beef and pastrami. They both seemed awful.

I remember watching my father collapse on our sofa in front of our bay window, right in front of our next-door neighbors. My father was strong. He was a physically big man. I remember him heaving and sobbing and his shoulders crumpling, and I was desperate for him to stop. *What is he doing?* I couldn't understand how he was letting people see him in that condition. I wanted my father to comfort me, but everyone was comforting him. He was emasculating himself. If he was losing it, then whatever we had left as a family was slipping away. We were unmoored.

Even though Chet was the leader of the kids, my dad was the leader of the family. He wore the pants, and you did what he said and he set the tone—and he was foundering. I looked at my dad's best friend, Jay Gaidemak, and I remember thinking that I wanted him to be my father—maybe because he wasn't crying. Maybe I was attracted to that. I don't remember. *We are now five, not six.* We were over.

I remember our relatives looking with pity at my father. I hated that. They already thought we were misfits or vagabonds, and *now this?*

I liked attention, but I didn't like this kind of attention. I didn't want pity. It was weak. My father was being weak. I remember that the word "professional" kept popping into my brain—my father was being *unprofessional.* How on earth was I going to be able to restore any dignity to this family I was born into? Now we were outcasts and we were victims. I could deal with being outcasts because I had Chet. He was never an outcast. Everyone loved Chet. My dad was an outcast, and now he was acting like a victim. He was making victims out of all of us. I stared at him hard with my eyes. *Stop this. You're making a spectacle of us.*

. . .

The subject of buying a family plot came up. My dad wanted to buy other plots next to my brother so that he and my mother could be buried next to him. I remember my parents talking to our rabbi about having an open casket even though my brother's body had been badly damaged and . . . something about his chest and forehead being caved in, and Jews didn't typically have open-casket funerals, but my mother was demanding it.

"He's my son, and I want to say goodbye to him," she told the rabbi. I remember these words exactly because I had never seen my mom demand anything from anyone. My father looked at my mother when she said that, and I remember thinking he had never seen her demand anything either. For the first time in my life, in that moment, my mother was more in control than my father.

The rabbi was telling my father that in order to be buried in a Jewish cemetery, my mother would have to convert to Judaism. *Wait, what?* I thought my mom was Jewish—mostly because no one ever told me she wasn't. During all of my brothers' and sisters' bar and bat mitzvahs, my mother would go up on the bimah and speak

Hebrew just like all the other Jewish mothers did during everyone else's bar and bat mitzvahs. She even went with my father and me to temple some Friday nights.

Apparently, my mother was Mormon, and when she came over from Germany to marry my father, she agreed to raise their children Jewish. I had never heard the word "Mormon" before. I always thought that when my dad called my mom a "shiksa," he was talking about her being German. I didn't know that "shiksa" meant a non-Jew. *Didn't your mother have to be Jewish in order for you to be Jewish? Was I not Jewish either? More great news.*

. . .

There was a funeral, and all I remember were my brothers Glen and Roy taking turns holding me in their laps as we all sat and cried throughout the service. I remember think-ing, *Why say such a thing if you didn't mean it? Why not be extra careful when you're on a fucking mountain peak if you promised your littlest sister that you would spend the rest of the summer tipping her over in a sailboat? Why would you break that promise to her?* I was livid.

I remember my German grandfather, Vati, coming over and saying to Roy: "You're the oldest now. You need to take care of your brothers and sisters." I remember thinking, *Roy isn't the oldest. There is no oldest anymore. We are a pot without a lid.*

They'd had to pump Chet's body with embalming fluid so that his face could be viewed. He looked dead and bloated. The funeral ended, and I guess at some point we went back to Martha's Vineyard to finish out our summer? I don't remember.

The day after the funeral must have been around the time that I stopped crying in front of people. If everyone in my family was going to fall apart—and the only person who held our shit together just let himself go off and die after he promised me that he would come back after his trip—then I would have to be strong on my own.

From that day onward, if I saw my mother crying or heard my parents groaning in anguish in their bedroom in the early hours of the morning, I would leave the house and get on my bike. I would ride my bike for hours and cry, but I would not allow myself to cry in front of anyone else or show any weakness. I would not talk about my brother to my family. If his name came up, I left the room and went for a bike ride. I would ride and ride and cry and cry and then walk back in the front door numb, hoping no one was there. No one being home was better than anyone being home.

. . .

At some point on the Vineyard that summer, my mother was standing on the deck looking at the water saying she was just waiting for a dream or a sign that Chet was okay—something from God. She wanted Chet to tell her he was safe and in heaven. She was trying to recruit me. That's how it felt when she tried to talk to me about Chet. It felt like she was trying to trick me into crying. I walked away from her and told her that there was no God and there was no heaven and out of everyone in the world she should know that by now.

My mother was in pain, and I chose to stab her again. I couldn't understand anyone else's pain—I couldn't even understand my own. I was confused, and I was mad. I remember thinking, *If Chet ever comes back, I'm not just going to go back to the way things were before.* No, I was going to punish him for what he did.

I remember asking my dad—who would sit for hours on the deck staring at the bay—if he would take me swimming.

My dad taught me how to swim when I was two or three. Whenever he was on the Vineyard—he commuted back and forth to New Jersey in the summer for nonexistent "used-car business"—he would carry me down from the house to the bay and hold me in his arms as he walked us into the water, and then I would swim with him on his back and climb on top of his shoulders and dive over the top of his head. I'd swim back to him holding my breath underwater, until I was right back in his arms. I loved swimming with my dad. After that, he would carry me up the path back to our house and tell me that I was stronger than anyone else he knew and that I'd probably end up competing in the Olympics.

My father didn't respond the first time, so I asked him a second time.

"We're not going in the water," he growled. "How can I go in the water, when my boy is dead?" His face was always contorted back then. Wretched. It hurt to look at both my parents.

I knew it was a risk to defy my father, but I was desperate for him to snap out of it. There was absolutely no light in him, and it was sucking the life out of what was left of the rest of us.

If I could just get him into the water, I knew he would relax a little or find a little ray of sunshine, or at least I could hold on to his back and then trick him into a hug. I just wanted him to breathe—I wanted to breathe too. The water was safe, because if I started crying I could just dunk my head and shake it off. If anyone could get him to experience some joy, it would be me.

I turned away from him and defiantly walked down the steps and across the lawn to the path that led down to the water. I never looked back, because I was scared shitless about how he would react to seeing me swim alone. The only rule I had growing up was never to swim alone.

I thought about getting spanked in the water and how funny that would be for both of us, him trying to catch me in the water to spank me. We'd both end up laughing so hard, I'd inevitably pee, and then I'd know my dad was mine. I could always get everyone in my family to laugh. I would just pee in my pants. That got everyone, every time.

When I got down to the water I nervously swam out about twenty yards. When I mustered up the courage, with every kind of fear pulsating through my body for having defied him, I looked back and saw he had gone inside.

. . .

I haven't had a bowl of cereal since that night in the kitchen with my brother. My brothers and sisters continued eating cereal all the time growing up. I didn't understand that— how they could do something that Chet loved so much, knowing what we knew. I didn't understand it because I was only able to draw from my own experience and didn't have the faculties to grasp that their relationships to cereal weren't as linked to Chet as mine was. That not everyone has your history or your past. That my brothers and sisters had their own memories of Chet, which didn't involve cereal, or even me. That each person has their own individual memory of the way things happened, and that you can waste so much time being angry at cereal.

I only ate eggs after Chet died. I've spent the past thirty-three years looking at cereal with disdain. Cereal was for children. Cereal was for nine-year-olds before they got their hearts broken. Cereal was off-limits.

. . .

One day, when I was around fifteen, I went foraging through the attic and found the pictures of my brother, head caved in, crumpled among rocks. I saw the pictures most parents would have made a better effort of hiding. His head, his chest, everything was crushed. Blood splattered the rocks above him. His limp body with his torn flannel shirt and jean shorts.

The mountain rangers and paramedics said he would have died instantly. *Lucky for him*, I thought, looking at those photos. The rest of our pain was taking forever.

TAMMY
TIME

There are many things dogs can do to make you feel like a better human being—like run toward you. For the record, I'm not one of those people who cares more about animals than humans, but I am someone who knows that loving a dog makes you a kinder and fuller person.

I don't have such luck with babies—and the feeling is mutual—so when I realized dogs were receptive to me, I returned the favor. My obsession with Chow Chow mixes came alive only when I rescued Chunk and was told he was a Chow mix. After six years, I decided it was time for Chunk to have a sibling. If Chunk was my firstborn, then Tammy was the stepdaughter that I loved *almost* more than my own blood. Tammy was a tramp, and that's what I respected about her the most.

The minute I saw her, I knew she was my dog. First, she

was a Chow mix and she had the purple tongue to prove it. Second, everything about her screamed Guadalajara. She looked like she had survived more than one street fight, and possibly one with an animal that wasn't a dog. She had one dead ear, alopecia on her ass, a very scantily clad tail, and a gait that hinted she had withstood hip-replacement surgery. Tammy was essentially a build-a-bear, and I knew that with some maternal attention from my cleaning ladies and some serious nutrition, I could turn that gait into a swagger. She was exactly the type of dog who could pull off an ear piercing.

We rescued Tammy from a facility in Long Beach—where, for the record, my cousin Molly said the following: "You can't get that dog. She's the ugliest one here."

I didn't think she was ugly. I thought she gave new meaning to the term "underdog." There was nothing ugly about her—scrappy, maybe, like she could have been carrying a pocketknife. She needed me, and whatever her name would turn out to be, I knew I needed her right back.

Even though Molly is twelve years younger than I am, she's smarter and more capable than I'll ever be, but in this particular instance I knew I had the ability to see what would be overlooked by most everyone else. That's the great thing about Molly: she knows I'm right about the things that get me in the gut. If I want to give a stranger $10,000 and she thinks they're going to spend it on crack—just because I met that person in a crack den—I will defer to Molly. She'll say something along the lines of, "Let's sleep on that, and if you still feel that way in the morning, then we'll do it and you'll have my full support."

That means no.

In this instance, Molly knew I meant business. I was rescuing Tammy and was going to give her what she needed—some real-life pampering. Someone to show her she was special. After all, when I get dogs, they aren't just being rescued by me, they are getting the love and attention of my cleaning ladies, my assistants, my dog walker, and everyone else who either works at my house or meanders through it on a regular basis.

Older dogs are special because they have had more rejection. Their hope is gone and, even though no one seems to know exactly how old any rescue dog is, when you adopt an older dog you are cramming their last years with love and giving them the security that comes with knowing they have a home. I have always believed you can erase bad memories with twice as many good ones. Maybe "erase" isn't the right word. Maybe "dim" is a better word.

After the people at the rescue center cleaned up Tammy, the two women handling her adoption told me that she could be a really beat-up four-year-old or she could be twelve, and that I should ask my vet for clarification when she had her first checkup. When the rescue presented Tammy to us, they had placed a little pink bow in each ear—the full-bodied ear and the limp one. She looked like a harlot. Once we got her in the car on our way home, we removed those embarrassing gender labels from her ears and got down to business.

"I feel like we have two names to choose from," I told Molly on our way back to my house. "Bernice or Tammy."

"Or Destiny," Molly said, with the dog sitting on her lap looking at the 405 freeway in awe. "Destiny is totally underused."

The first night I had Tammy home I had some people over for dinner. I picked her up and placed her in my lap, facing me, leaving both of her curiously stiff front paws positioned around each of my hips. Mary craned her head over the dinner table, amazed, and said, "Is she hugging you? I've never seen a dog do that."

"Chelsea's making her," Molly told Mary. I wasn't making Tammy do anything. I was showing her the seating options available to her, and one option was on my lap, facing me. Chunk would never sit on my lap—a) he was just too big, and b) he valued his personal space. I had finally found someone who didn't.

Tammy's teeth looked like she was from London, so when Tanner took her to her first vet appointment for a once-over, the nurse called and told me she may need to have all her teeth removed.

"Why would that be necessary?" I asked.

"Because they could all be infected," she informed me.

"Well, isn't there a way to tell which ones are infected first—before removing them all?"

"We won't really know until we put her under and take a look."

"How will she eat with no teeth?"

"Well, we won't take out any teeth that aren't infected," she assured me.

I was confused by this exchange. It felt like I was talking to a real live animal on the phone. "I don't want any teeth that aren't infected to be removed. Is that clear? Otherwise, I can just take her to my own dentist on Monday."

Poor Tammy. I wasn't about to let her move to Bel-Air with no teeth.

Before the dog nurse hung up, I asked if they had been able to decipher Tammy's age from her teeth's state of affairs.

"She could be anywhere from four or five . . . to twelve. It's hard to say."

Is it written somewhere in the *Journal of Medicine for Dogs* to just say that all rescue dogs are between the ages of four and twelve? How can it be that a swab of saliva can determine a dog's genetic heritage yet there isn't a more precise way to determine the age of a dog at this juncture in modern society?

. . .

Tammy would allow me to do almost anything to her body, and I needed her to know that she was going to get so tackled with love that her past would become a distant memory replaced by doggy massages, acupuncture, and baton twirling. She would let out a low rumble growl and I would go in closer, waiting for her to bite my face off, but she never once bit me. She bit my sister Shana once, but we all agreed that it was warranted. Tammy knew I was her captor and that it was in her best interest to just lean in and accept my devotion. Once I was done showering her with affection, she'd give me a final look to confirm that I was done molesting her, then scurry off the bed and down her doggy steps into the doggy bed that she'd usurped from Chunk. Once comfortably inside her new bed, she'd let out a groan that implied, *Thank God that's over.*

I couldn't keep my hands off her. I'd put her in a seatbelt in my lap on the way to work, when I knew she'd be much happier sitting in the backseat with her limbs free and one dead ear out the window. I can be an effusive lover, and after our initial trial period together, she just learned to deal with my advances.

She was just big enough for it to be imprudent to pick her up, but that didn't stop me either. She would immediately stiffen up, with her legs outstretched as if she were standing—making her look stuffed. She was a taxidermist's dream.

Chunk was slim, but I'm not sure how to describe Tammy's body. It seemed possible that some of her organs had shifted during one of her bar fights and then solidified. Her bald spots filled out within weeks, and her ratlike tail became full-bodied within her first month at home. She looked like an ad for nutrition.

She even started following me onstage during the interview segment of my Netflix show and would sometimes prop herself up on the little table between the guest and me. She didn't give a shit what anyone thought about her; she just wanted to make sure we were in the same room, nothing more, nothing less. She would have been fine if I never pampered or pet her, but like most rescue dogs, if I walked out of the room, she'd follow me. If I walked into a bathroom, she would open the door with her nose and stare at me until I was done. Chunk did the same thing in a more needy way. He'd open the bathroom door, or if we were at work, he'd slide headfirst under the bathroom stall and then avoid eye contact. Tammy would do these things, but with confidence. Where Chunk was refined, Tammy was street. She'd sit down in front of the toilet, face-to-face, as if to say: *Bitch, you need me more than I need you.*

I'm just keeping an eye on things. Tammy was more like a security guard.

She wasn't quite as spry as Chunk, so I didn't bring her on trips with me because she couldn't hop on and off planes and helicopters, but she was mentally fit, so there was backlash. That's what led me to get a third dog; I thought another dog would help distract Tammy from the fact that Chunk and I were traveling around the world. I didn't want her to feel excluded, since she was smart enough to hold a grudge.

My friend Kate—who loves animals more than people— texted me a picture of a dog that was at a rescue in Westwood, with a message that read, "This guy needs a home and he's part Chow Chow." This is what people do when they want me to rescue dogs; they tell me they are part Chow.

I went down to the rescue in Westwood and picked up our new dog. The girls working there told me he could be anywhere between four and twelve. I brought our new family member home and decided his name would be John. He was sweet and goofy and was definitely a big puppy—I figured he was probably two.

That night, in an effort to not overthink assimilating my new brood, I put all three dogs in my bedroom, and popped an edible. I was awakened by a low rumble that rose to a roar, and then to something that sounded like there was a werewolf nearby. When I flipped the lights on, Tammy's midsize, corpulent body had somehow wrapped itself around John's, like a contortionist. Thank God for instinct, because I'm scared to think what I would have done had I given it any thought. I screamed "No!" and then ripped Tammy off him. Her eyes were red and she looked like she was wearing red lipstick. I tossed her toward my closet. John was a bigger dog and stronger than I thought, and I couldn't hold him back from barreling toward her, so I dove right into the middle of them, grabbed Tammy, pushed her headfirst into my closet, and shut the door. Then I scurried to my feet in my staple sleepwear—a bra and thong—and fended off John, who was growling with his nose to the closet. Once I got him outside my room and closed the door, I sat down on my bed and thought I was going into cardiac arrest. I was gasping for breath as I tried to figure out what to do next. I was scared of both dogs at that point—I didn't know what they were capable of after seeing Tammy basically shape-shift into an anaconda.

When I moved my hand to my chest to try to self-soothe, I realized my bra had been torn open and one of my breasts had been set loose and was bleeding. I looked over at Chunk, who at some point during the altercation had wrapped himself inside the drapes.

I don't want to call Chunk a pussy, and I don't want to call Tammy a cunt, but I want to just throw those two words out there.

I called Molly and told her that I was living with a real-life Cujo, and even though I knew it was Tammy's fault, I was scared to open the door and check on John.

"I'll come get him," Molly said. It was 12:30 A.M., and while I waited for the coast to be clear, I texted Brandon to scan the security cameras in the morning and save whatever footage had just been captured for the next time me and my friends did mushrooms.

. . .

John never made the cut, because Tammy took him to task. Chunk knew better than to fight over territory he'd conquered long ago. He knew he belonged with me, but he understood there would be random dogs coming in and out of our lives, just the way people did.

. . .

Tammy was with me for three years and died shortly after the inauguration in January 2017. She felt the same way I did about Donald Trump. Molly and I were in South Africa at the time, and I got the call while Molly was out getting gifts for her brothers and sisters. She came back to the hotel room where I was sitting in a chair feeling guilty about traveling so much and not spending more time at home with Tammy.

"You gave her a good life, Chels," Molly said, hugging me. "No one else would have ever adopted that dog. Do you know how much shorter her life would have been if you'd been home more? And, don't forget, she brought me Hodor.*"

After Tammy died, I had some friends over for a small memorial service at my house, where we watched the video footage from my security cameras the night of the attack. It was the first time I had seen the crime scene, and Brandon had scored it to the theme song of *Rocky*. In it,

---

* Which is what Molly renamed John. As it happens, John/Hodor wasn't part Chow at all. Molly did his DNA testing and found out he is a purebred Leonberger. For the record, Tammy's testing revealed she was a Keeshond/Shepherd mix with a tiny bit of Chow. So, my obsession with Chows comes from being misinformed time and time again that they are the breed I am rescuing, not from ever actually having one.

you can see Tammy actually airborne after I got her off of John. The four teeth that I had campaigned for Tammy to keep ended up biting me in the tit. If I hadn't busted my nut with my topless photo rampage years before, this video would have been released on all of my social media platforms, on a loop.

Watching the video of Tammy alone, pacing in my closet like a large brown bear, reminded me what a force of nature she was. She was an underdog and a badass. She was a fighter, and even though I don't spend much time looking in the rearview mirror, my biggest regret is not ever getting her ears pierced.

SEYMOUR

In our next session, Dan told me about self-defining relationships—the critical relationships that are formative, that determine the person you become. The relationships that, if they were to go away, would change you. You would never recover from the loss.

"So, everything goes back to Chet? Really?" I asked Dan. "That seems too obvious."

"How do you mean?"

"Like, too easy. Is it really that simple? Am *I* really that simple?" Although it was a relief, at the same time it seemed like another cliché. *Of course, that's how simple this has always been.*

"Well, it sounds twofold to me. It sounds like you had one injury when your brother died, which you've said you've never properly addressed, and the second trauma was the retreat of the rest of your family, your father especially. Let's talk more about that."

"I don't remember much about those first few years after Chet died, other than that I had tons of problems at school. I became 'trouble.'"

"Did you have 'trouble' at school before your brother died?" Dan asked me.

"I don't really recall, but now that we're talking about it, how much trouble could I have gotten into before the age of nine? It's not like I was Satan. I think it was partly because my parents were so unreliable, so I think other parents wanted to avoid them, and partly because the attention I used to get at home had disappeared, and in response to that, I tried to get attention in other ways at school—however I could—which resulted in me constantly having to stay after school and sit in detention, and then, one by one, I was ostracized by all the friends I had in elementary school. Not because of my brother's death, but because I had turned into someone else."

Every once in a while I would self-analyze just to show Dan that I wasn't a complete moron and also to surprise myself with what I'd known all along but had never said out loud.

My sister Simone and my brother Glen became my de facto parents after Chet died—or at least they were a more reasonable version of parents. I think Roy had gone off to live in Miami or something. He smoked a lot of pot, and needed a place he could do that without my father screaming at him all the time. Shana was there, but for some reason I don't really remember her during that time.

But how much parenting could they have provided, really? Glen and Simone were both in college at Emory University, and anytime there was a crisis at home—of which there were many—one of them, usually Simone, had to manage it by phone from Atlanta. The crisis usually consisted of my father and me going to battle about the trouble I was in at school, my not listening to anything he or my mother told me, and my general lack of respect for anyone in a position of authority.

I became terrible. I hated everyone and everything. Shoving any pain in my pocket, hoping that eventually it would form a hole and fall out onto the street during one of my bike rides. I remember being on those bike rides, sailing past our neighbors' houses so fast that the tears were blowing off my face. *This is what the adults should be doing,* I thought, *figuring out a way to handle the situation without falling apart.* I would force myself up the hills around our neighborhood on my banana-seat bicycle and think, *You need to get stronger. Strength is what everyone in this family is missing—I'll probably have to start lifting weights.* I was dancing farther and farther away from myself.

I learned from Dan that being in motion was a way for me to avoid sitting still with my feelings. You can't let anyone see you cry, so you move.

Action is motion—is doing. Sitting is being. I had been a doer my entire life. I never sat still long enough to let anyone unglue my pain.

Dan wanted to know more about my father.

. . .

The best way to describe my father is that he's a lot like Donald Trump, but less successful, thank God—otherwise, the damage he could have unleashed on innocent people could have been more widespread. I would use the word "shyster" to describe my father. He claimed his entire life that if his own father hadn't died and left him a gas station, he'd be a civil rights attorney or a famous poet. "My father respected civil rights just about as much as he respected a hot pastrami sandwich," I told Dan. Based on his confused facial expression, I put it in less abstract terms. "If one's body is a temple, my father's body is an IHOP. I don't know much about his poetry, because—well, he's not a famous poet, that's why."

I organized my thoughts and opinions of my father in the most succinct way I could, hoping to give Dan a clear overview without shocking him.

"He's very nontraditional, and you'll probably be alarmed by some of the things you hear—at least that's my hope. Also, he wasn't abusive. Verbally, at times, but not physically. He definitely spanked me a few times when I was little and smacked me across the face a couple of times when I was too old to be spanked, but that stopped when I finally hit him back one day. I would also like to add that I deserved to be hit."

One can argue that no child deserves to be hit, but a slap across the face once or twice in your life sends a strong message, and the reason I don't have children is partly because of my belief in sending a strong message to people when they are assholes, and lots of kids are assholes.

I went on to tell Dan about going with my father to

Friday night services at temple, which used to be our thing when I was a little girl. My mom let me dress up in whatever ridiculous outfit I wanted, which was usually a combination of anything hot pink combined with red. I thought for a long time those two colors were great together, until later in life when I fashioned the phrase "summer whore" to describe that very look. My mom would slap some tights on me for good measure, and my father and I would go on our date night.

After Chet died, my dad didn't want to go to temple, but my mother somehow convinced him that I needed to go, which was silly in the sense that I had no regard for religion. Temple was about me being my dad's favorite. None of the older kids ever wanted to go to temple on a Friday night, because they had more interesting things to do.

If I could get him to temple, he would have to hold hands with me—that was our jam when I was a little girl. I'd get dressed up, and he'd show me off to the congregation, and then when the rabbi would ask one of the kids to answer whatever question he posed to the congregation, I'd raise my hand, and the rabbi would always call on me—probably because no other kids raised their hands. Then I'd run up to the bimah, and the rabbi would pick me up, and I'd whisper into his ear, "I don't know," really loudly. Then the whole congregation would laugh, and I'd run back to my father, and he'd put me in his lap, and we would both be beaming.

But, now that I was nine or ten, I wasn't so little, so my outfits were no longer cute—I looked more like a child prostitute—and the only person who still was physically able to pick me up had gone off and let himself die. Temple was a disaster that night because everyone in the synagogue was coming up to my father and telling him how sorry they were about Chet. *Fuck,* I remember thinking. *When were people going to get over this already?* I was trying to get my father back to some sort of routine, and all these people kept interrupting my progress.

There were cookies after every Friday night service, so afterward, I excused myself to go collect them and bring some back home for my mother. When I came back to look for my dad, I couldn't find him anywhere and I started to panic. I ran back and forth through all the rooms in the temple in search of him. *Where was he? Did something happen? No, no, no.*

My panic turned to hysteria. A woman I knew from temple saw me and came over to me and tried to calm me down. I hadn't cried in front of anyone for months, so it was more like hyperventilating. Not being able to breathe, but not crying. Like the girl in *Jaws,* who saw her boyfriend get eaten by the shark and was left out to sea for hours until Roy Scheider found her inside the sailboat curled up in a ball, in shock.

More people were gathering around, and then a woman kneeled down in front of me, put her hands on my shoulders, and told me to breathe. Then someone in the crowd whispered to someone else that he had seen my father leave moments earlier and that he seemed out of it. He had driven home without me.

I wanted to die right then and there. I remember telling the people standing around me that I was fine to walk home. I don't even know if I knew how to get home from temple at that age. Plus, it would have been nine P.M. on a Friday night. *Maybe I'd get hit by a car and then my father would have no choice but to wake up. Two dead kids. That would teach him.*

The rabbi came over, and I remember seeing him in plain clothes without his Jewish garb on and wondering if he was going to take me home with him and if I would just become part of his family. He wouldn't forget to pick me up, and his clothes were clean and pressed, and he seemed so normal—like a professional. Professionals showed up when they were supposed to. *Why couldn't my dad just be more professional?*

Instead, the rabbi drove me home, and when we got to our house, my dad's car was in the driveway, and our rabbi walked me to the front door. "Your dad is in a lot of pain, Chelsea," he said. "I know you must be too."

"I just have a stomachache," I told him. "I'm fine."

"If it's okay with you, I'm going to come inside and talk to him."

"Okay," I said.

I opened the front door, which was always left unlocked, and all the lights were off. *Of course.* Everyone was asleep.

I needed to recover these optics quickly. "He's just sick," I told the rabbi as we stood in the darkness of our front hallway. "He's got a heart condition, and sometimes he gets heart attacks."

My rabbi kissed me on the forehead and said something in Hebrew that I didn't understand.

. . .

Dan told me to stop talking. To sit with the feeling of my father driving home without me. Sitting with my feelings meant it was time to cry again.

I wondered how many more sessions would be like this. It was fucking exhausting, and our sessions were in the morning, which meant I'd show up to work for hair and makeup looking like I had just gotten into a fight with a cherry snow cone.

I put myself through this because it was a psychological workout. It was easy to not address my own issues and to focus on everyone else's. Judging other people had become my way of avoiding judgment of myself, and I had to do better than that. Going back to Dan week after week, knowing that I was stripping away all the layers of protection I had spent years fortifying, was particularly dreadful. I knew it was worth continuing. If you went to the gym every day, you were going to get stronger; this was my mental gym.

"Also," I added, when I felt like enough time had passed, "my parents did this kind of shit all the time. They'd forget to pick us up from Hebrew school, or regular school, and it wasn't just me. It happened to my brothers and sisters before I was born, so I don't think we can blame this on Chet. My sister Simone went to school with the three older boys for an entire week when she was four years old, because my mom thought you could just do that. She didn't really understand how things worked in this country."

"What do you mean? Where was she from?"

"She was German, but she was fluent in English. That wasn't the problem. She was just so laissez-faire about everything. The school called her and told her that Simone wasn't old enough for kindergarten and they couldn't allow her to keep coming. You have to understand that my parents were not equipped for or interested in conventional parenting. They were *off*, and they were like that before Chet died. My dad worked when the older kids were growing up, and I guess my mother was usually asleep, so it was always mayhem. It probably was worse for me because the older kids were all gone, and that was after my dad had sold the gas station and worked from home, which meant he had a big oak desk with a lot of papers on it that meant nothing, and a big room he called his 'office.' Oh, and he had a fax machine. He never shut the fuck up about that either. He'd tell waiters at restaurants that they could fax him the bill—as if that were ever an option in any sort of reality, ever. He also used a toothbrush to comb my hair when I couldn't find a hairbrush one morning before school and my mom was away somewhere. I just want you to know the kind of operation my parents were running."

"Was your mother depressed?"

"Maybe, but she also just loved to sleep. My grandmother—who was a Nazi, by the way—would always tell the story that the teacher at my mother's school in Germany used to find her taking naps underneath the staircase every afternoon. She just loved sleeping. Our whole family can sleep for hours, especially when we're all together. Either we bore the shit out of one another or it's genetic. I can sleep for fourteen hours straight. With a Xanax, twenty."

"We can talk about the Xanax later. Was your grand-mother really a Nazi?"

"No, not really, but she was in Germany during the war, so she was complicit. Like Ivanka."

"Okay, back to your father."

"Right. After that, my father and I couldn't be in the same room for a long period of time without screaming at each other. All I wanted to do was get out of the house and stay out of the house, and all my father seemed to want to do was force me to sit at home and punish me."

"What was he punishing you for?"

"Everything and nothing. He just hated me. Well, I mean, I know he didn't *hate* me, but that's what it felt like."

"And what did *that* feel like?" Dan leaned forward, his forearms on his knees, hands clasped.

"I just told you, Miracle-Ear. Like he hated me." I didn't call Dan "Miracle-Ear," but I thought about it.

"But what did that feel like?"

Dan did this a lot. Asked me a question I had already answered.

He wanted me to understand that the outward feeling was not the only feeling. He pushed me to identify what was underneath that feeling, which was anger, and then sadness, and then rejection. I felt alone. That I couldn't rely on anyone but myself. Helpless.

Now, I know that my stubbornness was patrilineal— that it came directly from the person who had withdrawn his affection. If he still loved me, he wasn't about to tell me, and I surely wasn't going to ask him to love me. Two obstinate assholes reeling in pain. Things could have been so much easier if we had just had the ability to reach out to each other.

"Our signals were always crossed," I told Dan. "None of us had the tools."

"That's why you're here," he told me. "To get the tools."

"I definitely remember loving my father before Chet died, and not loving him after, so there's that," I added.

"Well, you probably loved him still, but you were hurt, and it sounds like you turned that hurt into anger, because, as I said, anger is motion, and it allows you to avoid sitting with your feelings. In a sense, you felt that your father had broken up with you too. That must have been really scary for a little girl."

Getting broken up with twice by the age of nine. I had never looked at it that way.

"Yeah, that's a lot of male rejection before I even got my period."

Two guys in the span of one year, and I hadn't even started dating. I had on no occasion thought about my experiences within this kind of framework, or thought about how my father must have felt losing his firstborn son. Of course he was wrecked. Who wouldn't be? Why would he have any inkling about how to handle losing a child? No one has any idea what to do with that news.

"That must have been when I realized I needed to grow myself up. To become a fixer."

"Probably," Dan agreed. "No one helped you with your pain, you were too young to deal with it on your own, and it sounds like when everyone around you disengaged, your pain turned into anger, which turned into motion, and from everything you're telling me, you haven't stopped moving since."

"Yeah, that sounds about right. I just needed him, and he had this terrible habit of showing up only at times when I didn't want him to. Like at school, I just didn't want him representing me."

"Why not?"

"Because he was loud and mostly disheveled. His outfits were the casual equivalent of what I wore to temple on Friday nights. I just believed I was better at advocating for myself. Plus, my mom was sweet and quiet and I wanted more people to see her, to see that I had a mother that was like other mothers—one who showed up."

"How did that feel?"

"Lonely."

Most days in elementary school, I could easily walk to school and back by myself, but the winter weather required transportation by car, and since my parents didn't want to deal with that, they farmed me out to our neighbor. In exchange for a ride to school on winter mornings, my parents offered up my math-tutoring services to their second grader, Samson. Even though I was in the fourth grade at the time, I shouldn't have been tutoring anyone in any subject—least of all math. After a few weeks, it became apparent that Samson was smarter than I was, and that's when he and I got philosophical and just started playing Super Mario Bros.

I remember walking home from Samson's house one

afternoon around five P.M. and being asked by my father, in one of his bouts of selective parenting, where I'd been.

"The zoo," I told him, and walked into the kitchen to see if my mom had cooked anything.

"Did you have a field trip?" my mom asked sweetly, standing with her back to me, over the stove.

"No, I just went on my own," I told her. *As if a nine-year-old had the wherewithal to take a day trip to the zoo, solo.*

My father went back to reading the newspaper and my mother asked me if I was hungry. I was always hungry, so I took a bowl of whatever she was making and walked upstairs to my room, where I could at least be consistent with the company I was keeping.

I wanted someone to look after me—someone who would ask where I'd been. I wanted a mother who wanted other kids' parents' phone numbers. I wanted parents who didn't bounce checks. I wanted to be picked up from Hebrew school on time—or at all—in a car with four doors that opened and closed.

I wanted to escape, to go away to boarding school, anything to get away from my father and all the friends I had lost. My parents couldn't afford boarding school; otherwise they would have been glad to send me. They were just as tired of me as I was of them. I would make my way through one group of friends and then move on to another, and when I was out of people, my parents would transfer me to a different school. I went from being a sweet and feisty and happy and spoiled little girl who just had to smile to get anything I wanted to being a girl who had the rug ripped out from under her, and everything she considered to be love taken away. I didn't understand what was happening, but I was so angry. I was losing my grip and flailing around, and I couldn't calm down long enough for anyone to help me, because I really didn't believe anyone could. No one seemed reliable.

"I remember once sitting around for some family dinner. I must have been around thirteen. There weren't many of us there, just my parents and Shana, and I looked around the table thinking, *These are not my people.* I thought, *I'm going to have to branch out on my own at some point. Obviously, I'll keep in touch with these people who have had a hand in keeping me alive and feeding me, but this can't be my real family.*"

"And what did that feel like?"

"I think I wanted to reject them before they could reject me," I told Dan.

Dan asked me if my parents had any grief counseling or if they took any of us to therapy. This was laughable. They didn't know anything about therapy or what responsible people did when their children died. They thought a parent-teacher conference was a social mixer for adults—simply because it was at night—therefore, it made no difference whether they showed up or not.

"The subject of therapy never came up except for the time I woke up and pretended I couldn't move my legs."

"What was wrong with your legs?"

"I believe I was trying to avoid a German test that I had neglected to study for, but now that we're talking about this, I could have just feigned being sick, if that was the case, because my parents generally didn't challenge that. I remember saying something to my mom about having polio and her rolling her eyes at me, which made me work even harder at convincing her I had polio. I must have been thirteen or fourteen at the time."

At the emergency room that day, the doctor pricked my legs up and down with a needle while I pretended not to feel a thing—and when he was done, he drew the curtain to my examination room shut and suggested to my parents that I have a psychiatric evaluation. They brought me to three different therapists, but I refused to speak to any of them. I just sat there and grimaced and stared each one down until they gave up. Every therapist who gave up was another win. I was as stubborn as I needed to be, and when anyone around me gave up on me, I had won again. *They had failed the test. Another faker who pretended they cared but didn't really.*

Saying all of these incredibly embarrassing things out loud to someone made me feel sick, mostly. I thought about the absurdity of being forty-two years old and opting to get a psychiatric evaluation from a doctor, after telling him a story about getting a psychiatric evaluation from another doctor. *What . . . a full circle.*

"My father may as well have been dead at that point," I told Dan. "He was never the same after Chet died—none of us were—but he never really came back until years later, and then there was a good ten years of happier times."

"Tell me about that."

"I mean, I love him now, but it took a long time for us to reconnect. It wasn't until I moved to Los Angeles and came home to visit them. I would come home for a week during Christmas and a week in the summer, and my dad would pick me up at Newark Airport. I remember loving that. I would be so excited on the flight, and then running out to see him. He always had a great big reaction to seeing me—arms waving in the air, happy, smiling big."

As I recounted this to Dan, I remembered never having to wait for my father at the airport, other than for him to circle the area in order to avoid getting a ticket from the police. He always picked me up when I came home, and I never had to wait for him. I had forgotten that.

Dan was looking at me with the recognition of what I'd just discovered.

"He finally started showing up for me." I knew to sit with that before Dan had to tell me.

I had to leave my parents to love them again. I had to move across the country to appreciate that I actually had any pull toward them—that I needed them. I had to get away from them in order to come back to them. I'd like to say that they did the best that they could, but that couldn't have been their best. I wasn't doing my best either, so the idea that everyone is always doing the best they can is a trope. Some people are just interested in surviving; doing their best doesn't even occur to them.

I felt loved by my dad again, celebrated. He was impressed that I had moved to Los Angeles at nineteen, on my own, and was doing stand-up comedy, and he wanted to hear everything and anything about my life.

When I think back about that time, I am struck by my fearlessness, my drive, my ambition. It doesn't even feel like me now. I'm jealous of that girl. A girl with a plan. I

knew exactly what I was going to be, and I was right—
powerful. My intention broadsided any challenge that
came my way. I didn't care what anyone thought, what
anyone said, all I wanted was my own life, and I was going
to keep moving until I got it. I wanted to be a person people could depend on, and I was going to do it my way. You
would have to be young and stupid to believe that you are
going to move to Los Angeles to become famous, which is
exactly what it takes to achieve a fantasy—youth and stu-
pidity.

· · ·

I remember one summer flying into Newark Airport, my
parents picking me up in their gold Dodge Caravan and
driving the five hours up I-95 to catch the ferry from
Woods Hole to Martha's Vineyard. Why I didn't just fly to
Boston is a mystery because it would have saved me a car
ride with my parents that wasn't luxurious or alluring on
any level—so the only conclusion can be that I was se-
verely dehydrated for their attention. I wanted to be their
only focus, and for that five-hour car ride and subsequent
forty-five-minute ferry ride, that's exactly what I got.

I remember us pulling up to one of those McDonald's
rest stops on the way to the ferry, and I was tired and
cranky from my overnight flight, and also grossed out that
my parents still ate at McDonald's. They didn't even have
the decency to use the drive-through; they wanted to go in
and sit at a table like it was some sort of date night.

"Listen to this, Ritala," my dad said to my mom. "She's
been in California for less than two years, and she's already

turned against McDonald's—a perfectly decent establishment. You can't screw up breakfast, Chels; you just can't."

I remember walking in with them and scowling at the menu, wondering what I would be able to eat. My dad ordered two bacon-and-egg biscuits and ordered me an Egg McMuffin. The guy behind the cashier was a little slow on the uptake, and my dad's people skills were always a little gruff, unless you were an attractive woman, and then he was always nice. Like Donald Trump.

"Two coffees and one Diet Coke," he told the guy behind the counter.

The cashier was for some reason confused by the request for a Diet Coke in lieu of the coffee or orange juice that came with each breakfast meal, and it was taking longer than it should have, but I remember my dad's response.

"Listen, buddy, this isn't that difficult. It's breakfast, for Christ's sake, and you only have three options." Then he put both of his hands on the counter, cocked his head to the side, and said with complete seriousness and some concern, "Have you had all your testing done?"

"Have you had all your testing done?" was the single most ridiculous line I had heard my father ever say, and I turned on my heels to find the bathroom before I urinated on myself.

When I got back to the table, my mom and dad were sitting there eating their gross biscuits, while my dad separated my egg from the English muffin and placed the egg alone on the paper wrapper. Then he took out a cheap bottle of vodka and put it on the table.

"Here," he said. "We brought some vodka for the ride,

because we never know what kind of mood you'll be in." It was ten o'clock in the morning.

I would never drink the type of vodka my dad would purchase, because he knew nothing about vodka, but I do remember that's when I started loving my father again. My parents rarely drank, so for them to go to a liquor store and buy alcohol meant they had been paying attention after all. Separating my carbs from protein was the icing on the cake. They were back.

I lay down with my head in his lap in a booth at Mc-Donald's, looking at the paper bag of vodka, thinking, *So this is what it's like to be parented.*

"Chels, if we knew growing up that all you needed was a little vodka to calm you down, we would have started giving it to you as a baby," my dad said, patting me on my butt as if I were a nine-year-old.

"Yes, Chelsea," my mother chimed in. "Life could have been so much easier," she said, reaching over the table, pinching my nose.

I propped my head up off my dad's lap. "Had I known it would just take me moving across the country to get picked up on time, I would have moved to LA when I was twelve."

"How did that feel?" Dan asked me.

"Great. I felt like a little girl. I loved that morning at McDonald's."

• • •

That year on Martha's Vineyard and every year after I visited in the summer, I would get up at seven A.M., before any of the other kids were awake, and go out to breakfast with my parents. I think of that time, and our breakfasts in Edgartown, and I felt loved—like they were really getting to know me, and that they liked this young-adult version of myself. "Guts," my dad would say to me all the time. "My girl's got guts."

The burden of raising me had been lifted. I had gone off on my own to California and chosen to come back without the pressure of them having to prove themselves to me— and, finally, they seemed as close to being parents as they ever had.

It turned out we all just needed a break.

. . .

My dad has a great face. It's full of something you'd want to get involved with. He has the features of a black man, which is part of my affinity for it, but not all of it. His face represents his interest in things, his intelligence, his joy, his naughtiness. He's not cut off from things—he's not judgmental. He has always been a flirt. I like that in a guy. I love flirting. I loved flirting with my dad. He saw himself in me and that was enough for me, and really still is. I always wanted his admiration—and when I finally got it, I was in charge of our relationship, and our dynamic flipped. I became the taker-carer of things, the one who called the shots.

My dad is also the owner of a laugh that could light up an entire football field. When he laughs, he knows he's doing you a favor, because it heightens the mood and sets the tone. He has the power to take all the tension out of a room—usually tension he was responsible for creating in the first place—with one huge smile and a head tilt, and when he turned around a good corner, we all jumped on board without any need for an apology for the behavior that came before. We were just joyful to move on to the fun stuff, because if he was in a bad mood, everyone would be walking on eggshells.

His laughter was loud, and if you could get him going, he would throw his head back and howl, and then slam his hand on the dining room table, and it was infectious. No one laughs like that unless people are watching, but I never thought about that then.

In those moments, when he was wildly happy and playful, it was impossible to think of him as anything less than everything.

What a power to have to set the tone for an entire room. What a burden. To have that kind of power means you are responsible for every mood in the room. If everyone is scared of you, then you are the one in charge. I definitely know what that feels like, because the more I write about him, the more I realize how much I am him. I kind of respect my father when I think about him in broader and more forgiving terms. Back then he really didn't give a shit what anyone thought about him. Or maybe he did. I just know what I thought of him. He was a faker, but he was also a force of nature. No person is just one thing.

That's how I'm like my father. I know I'm always putting on a show. I like to be contagious. I love lighting up a room. I know how powerful that is and I revel in it. It's when I feel the most like myself. It makes me feel smart and charming—what my father probably felt when he did it. Glowing, beaming, self-satisfied.

All of my summer visits after I moved to California had that same tenor. They were all a bit idyllic, and more fun, and we were all adults, so there were boyfriends and girlfriends and spouses and babies, and the atmosphere in the house seemed ebullient again. My dad seemed ebullient again. He was never fully happy, because he is naturally very moody, but when he was on the Vineyard, we all felt the love.

He would always tell me I looked too skinny, which was silly because I've never been too skinny no matter which eating disorder I was testing out.

One night when we were all out to dinner, I whispered to the server that I wanted a double vodka on the rocks, and my dad chimed in.

"If you're going to order a double, you should do it loudly and with confidence. You like your vodka, Chels. That's your ameliorant. I'm your dad. I know my own child. You've got nothing to be ashamed of."

It was moments like that with my father that filled me with warm affection. Once I got older, I never really had to hide anything from him, because I felt how much he adored me again. His moods were not personal. They weren't about me, at least not anymore. I always knew when my father looked at me that he thought I was smart, that I was capable, and that anyone who was in my way better get out of the way because I was filled with conviction. That was his word for me: conviction. My word for him was the prefix of that word: *con*.

. . .

"Then he had quintuple-bypass surgery when he was in his late sixties, or seventy, maybe . . . anyway, and then it was all downhill after that."

"In what way?" Dan asked.

I came home early for Christmas one year in my mid-twenties because my dad had been rushed to the hospital the night before with chest pain, and they discovered that he had ninety percent blockage in all five of his main arteries. He would need surgery the next morning.

"My mom woke me up early the next morning. 'Chelsea, your father just called and said he wants to wait until the spring for his bypass surgery, so I'm going to go pick him up from the hospital.'"

I could have hit my mother right then and there. That was *so* my mother. So passive and so easily pushed around. It drove me mad. Only my father would think he could wait and schedule bypass surgery during a more pleasant time of year—as if he were scheduling a garden party. That's the kind of asshole I was dealing with.

I got out of bed and went into my mother's bathroom to brush my teeth. I used my parents' bathroom when I came home to visit, which was odd because their bathroom was a complete shitshow, a representation of my mother's "European-style" hygiene.

My mission was to get him into the operating room, and there was no other possible outcome. When I was running out the front door into the snow in our driveway— I was in some version of pajamas or sleepwear, and for some reason, I had thrown on my dad's Ugg boots—my mother asked if she should come, and I remember looking at her and thinking, *Definitely not.*

At the hospital I screamed and yelled and threw one of the biggest tantrums of all time, until he agreed to go into surgery. I fought so hard just to get a father I couldn't stand to stick around. My brothers and sisters were shocked that I had gotten him into surgery, because he could be so stubborn. They couldn't believe I had convinced him to do it. No one could convince my father of anything.

I had proven myself to be responsible. I had become someone you could rely on to get the job done. I liked that feeling a lot. My family knew I meant business that day, that I was dependable. The biggest fuckup in the family could do something none of them had even tried to do— guide a rhinoceros into an operating room. The surprise in Simone's voice filled me with pride.

"Okay, they just took him in."

"Took him in where?"

"To the OR."

"You're kidding me. How did you get him to do it?"

"I threatened him, mostly," I said, like a businesswoman. "He'll be in the OR for four to six hours. I need you to bring me some shoes—preferably my own." I looked down at my footwear. "Or some breath mints for Dad's Uggs. They smell like hard-boiled eggs."

I had become a fixer. A true number eight. I didn't think about how scared my father must have felt, or try to understand where he was coming from. I just needed to fix the situation for the family, and for myself. I thought about the choice between life and death, and there wasn't a chance that was going to happen to us again. *Not on my watch.*

I can't believe I convinced him to go through with a quintuple bypass just so he could go on to sexually harass the entire African American and Cuban communities of the tristate area. My brothers and sisters were kind enough to remind me of this every time he had another "incident."

. . .

My relationship with my father had always been about my version of things; I never contemplated what might have happened in his life to make him act the way he did. I never considered his story. I was a child, yes, but then I was an adult. It's hard for me to have sympathy for my father because a lot of his behavior I find inexcusable, but it's important for me to look at his story as independent from my own, and try to have a little empathy. I had never thought about being his child. I thought about him being my father, but never the other way around. Empathy. We both had none.

I didn't know he lost his gas station after working six nights a week, that he was held up at gunpoint, that he came home early every Wednesday night, with corned beef and pastrami sandwiches, because he wanted time with his family—that he worked fourteen-hour days. This was all before I was born. It was all before Chet died.

When Chet died, he was torn apart with grief, but he never gave up, never threw in the towel. He could have gone off and left us, or he could have just killed himself. He didn't do either of those things. I don't know if it was the best he could do, but I also don't know that it wasn't.

No person is just one thing. People can be filled with light and affection and also be tortured and conniving and dishonest. Happiness can coincide with great pain. One can lead while also following, the same way one can follow while also leading.

Dan asked me how all of this made me feel.

I told him that I now understood my father's limitations along with my own. I thought our relationship was about me showing him how great I was, when truly he was most likely trying to prove to me how great *he* was. He was wondrously obsessed with himself, as I was with his affection for me. Today I'm able to say with confidence that I do love my father. I don't know how much I like his behavior, but in the end, isn't love more valuable than like?

. . .

I had a boyfriend when I was eighteen years old. He was twenty-eight. He had a house in Belmar, New Jersey, and we would go there every weekend with my fake ID. He thought I was twenty because that's what I told him. Every Sunday, when we would drive home from the shore back to our respective suburban dwellings, I knew I wouldn't see him for a few days because we both lived with our parents, and sleepovers were a no-no—for his parents. I doubt mine would have noticed.

Every car ride, I fell silent, refusing to speak to him the whole way home because I hated that we would be separating. He would ask me every weekend what was wrong, but I didn't have the tools to express to him that I hated having to separate. That would have made me vulnerable, and vulnerability wasn't allowed. Eventually, he broke up with me because it was too hard for a twenty-eight-year-old to date a nine-year-old.

"I've been nine for a really long time," I finally said to Dan.

"Probably only with men."

"This is why I test them. If things are going well for a couple of weeks, I raise the stakes and force the person I'm dating to prove to me he loves me and that he is willing to do anything to demonstrate that. I create drama so that he can mollify the situation in the name of protecting me. I just really want someone to ask me where I've been all day."

"Of course you do. That's called a relationship."

Now that I had a better understanding of why I was so pissed off, I could finally do something about it. Not knowing where your anger is coming from is basically the same as walking through life with a broken leg. "It's fine," you tell people who are constantly looking at you with concern. "Nothing to see here."

· · ·

It wasn't until I met Dan that I realized Chet was my very first breakup. That my nine-year-old brain had no ability to distinguish between death and rejection. That my nine-year-old brain didn't understand that my brother didn't choose to die. That Chet didn't find another family with a little sister he liked more. That was simply the way my nine-year-old brain had digested it. I was reacting to the death of my brother like a spurned lover.

Subconsciously I was waiting for my brother to come

home because that's what he said he was going to do, and I waited every single day for that to happen, even when I had ostensibly accepted his death. To my nine-year-old brain, it was rejection.

I didn't know then that my brother's death was defining me. I didn't know that I had the ability to say no to being defined by death. Now I was with a person who could help me process what happened and turn the parts of me that acted like a nine-year-old into a self-actualized adult who had come to a better understanding of what it means to dig deep and admit your pain—thereby beginning the process of relinquishing it. I was in a place where my brother dying no longer had to define my existence. It's part of who I am—perhaps the biggest part—and it may have helped steer me in a certain direction, but it is not all of me.

I define me. No event or person does this. I define me. I decide who I am and how I'm going to behave, and I choose to be better. To look more carefully, to trudge deeper. To think about other people's pasts and not judge someone for doing or handling something differently than I would. To understand my limitations, my shortcomings—that is my growth edge.

CHUNK

Be careful of the people you make
fun of because you will most likely
turn into one of them.

After Tammy died, Chunk had a new spring in his step, as if five years had been added to his life. He was suddenly the picture of vitality. Chunk couldn't stand Tammy, and I didn't blame him. Tammy was a cunt to Chunk, and Chunk was too much of an existentialist to be bothered by Tammy's sophomoric chicanery. He stayed out of her way because he didn't want to rock the boat. I like to believe that when Tammy came home with me, Chunk thought, *Here we go, another one of these dime-store whore rescues. This floozy won't last a fortnight.* I don't know why I believe Chunk was British, but there's really no other explanation for his regality. Chunk was a prince.

If Tammy was my family mascot, Chunk was my husband. Everybody loved Chunk. His smooth soft hair, his well-mannered disposition. He didn't have the body type

I'm normally drawn to, but any parent will tell you none of that matters when it's your own flesh and blood. He gave our family some much-needed dignity. He was described by many as aloof, but that was also part of his charm. He had the disposition of a butler—he was congenial but kept his distance. Without a kerchief around his neck, he was just another well-groomed dog from Bel-Air. With the kerchief, he was cooler than Fonzie. He amassed a large social media presence during his time with us and never once used it for ill. He didn't troll people online or spread fake news. He was pure goodness. He loved me categorically, but that's not the only reason I loved him. It was most of the reason—but he also had qualities I didn't jibe with. When I came home drunk or stoned, he laid some heavy judgment on me. When I had friends over, he'd give me a look that said, *Lights out in five.* I tolerated it because he never said it out loud. He never diminished the meaning of his judgment with lectures. The stares stayed fresh. It made me feel I had a sort of spiritual guide—albeit a sober one. That is, until I got him his own marijuana pills. That's when the judger became the user.

. . .

Soon after I got Chunk, Molly and I took him on what we presumed was his first trip to the beach, but once we got there, it was clear he had been to a beach before—possibly even as a lifeguard. He sat in front of the water, listening to the waves crash with his eyes closed, while he let the wind blow through his hair—like Ernest Hemingway. Ernest Hemingway would probably have been blacked out, but for some reason that's who I always thought of when I watched Chunk on the beach. Molly said he reminded her more of Stevie Wonder at the beach, but Molly can be a contrarian. Whenever Chunk was in this state of tranquility, I wished he could drink and smoke cigarettes, but after many failed attempts, I had to accept that neither vices held any interest for him.

"Can you believe he loves the beach as much as I do?" I asked Molly.

"Yeah, because he lives in a fucking icebox. He's probably never felt the sun on his back."

I like my house cold, and if I've been drinking, I like it even colder. I've always held the false assumption that things with fur could easily withstand freezing temps. "I'm just kidding—his fur keeps him warm," Molly said to assuage my fear that I was torturing my own dog. "Poor thing thought he was going to become the Fresh Prince of Bel-Air, and instead he lives in the Arctic. He's like a modern-day Shackleton."

• • •

While on a self-imposed sabbatical between my shows at E! and Netflix, I decided it was time for Chunk to see Europe. My family and I were meeting in Spain for a week, and I believed that after years of North American travel and good plane etiquette, Chunk had earned himself the right to a trip overseas. I have an affinity for Spain because the food is delicious and the Spanish take lots of siestas. That is when I get my best work done—when whole towns are asleep.

Someone from Chunk's multipronged medical team had given him a prescription for sleeping pills. I was advised to give him as little water as possible on the day of our "journey," which seemed like sound advice for a fourteen-hour voyage—a ten-hour flight to Germany, a two-hour layover, and then a two-hour flight to Formentera. The German layover added a nice ancestral touch, since Chunk was half German Shepherd and half Chow. It would be his very own episode of *Who Do You Think You Are?* When we reached the Spanish island, Chunk would be reminded of my cleaning ladies and feel right at home.

The first leg to Germany was uneventful. Chunk sat at my feet during takeoff and I used him as a footstool. Once we were airborne and I was able to recline my seat into a bed, he hopped up, and I positioned him as a headrest. This configuration worked well in that he wouldn't be able to get up without waking me—and his breath would help keep me knocked out. (From this vantage point, I realized the two connected seats in the middle aisle of the first-class cabin would be an even better configuration, so I texted Brandon to purchase those two seats for our return flight, so that Chunk and I could return to our homeland like a real husband and wife.)

Chunk's breath got trickier as he got older. I had received multiple complaints from some of my closest friends, who pointed out that it was hot and strong—but to me it smelled like home. It also smelled like littleneck clams, but I'm a fan of littleneck clams. Chunk is also a fan of littleneck clams, which explained his breath—but I digress. The important part of this story is that I was able to tolerate Chunk's breath, which means I am capable of accepting people's shortcomings—but usually only if that person never speaks. Chunk had the only terrible breath I've ever loved. That's how I knew I was capable of unconditional love—his breath and his slender body. Neither was my first choice.

My vet warned me that the sleeping pill could make Chunk very thirsty—which, as usual, didn't add up. Why would I give him a pill that would make him thirsty during the only window of time when I wasn't allowed to give him water?

I decided to abstain from giving Chunk or myself a sleeping pill on the flight. That's what good parents do; they make sacrifices for their children. Chunk was a complete champ the entire way to Spain. We got up a couple times to do a lap or two, and when I had to use the restroom, I just tied his leash to my cup holder. People kept coming over and commenting on how well-behaved Chunk was—and on his looks, of course. People were always searching for the right word to describe him. Regal, debonair, rakish. Chunk was always polite with strangers, but never effusive. He would entertain a stranger with a smile and perhaps a paw shake, but he wouldn't be caught dead licking someone. He had too much dignity for that.

Once we got to Formentera, my sister Simone took him for his first long walk. When she came back she described it as a "disembowelment"—another reason I loved Chunk: saving his excrement for someone in my family. My brothers and sisters know I am not equipped to deal with any of the responsibilities that come with parenting, so they immediately take charge of my dependents. Likewise, Chunk knows it's better to go for a walk with anyone other than me.

. . .

Halfway through the trip, predictably, I became irritated with my family. I came home from a sailing excursion and took a closer look at Chunk's "meds." It's not often I come across a sleeping agent I'm unfamiliar with, but it does happen. I googled "alprazolam" and discovered that Chunk's medicine was just a generic form of Xanax. I could have high-fived myself if I had gotten more air. "It's doggy Xanax!" I exclaimed to my aunt Gaby, who was in the kitchen making everyone lunch. "This is a game changer."

My brother is married to a Russian woman with whom he bickers about almost anything—it could be a bicycle helmet. It is of my opinion that their three sons—my three nephews—are prisoners in their home, but that may be because I grew up in my home and can't relate to any kind of hands-on parenting. My sister-in-law is more than just hands-on—I believe she would actually live inside one of her sons' ears if she could. She is supremely overprotective and consumed with everything from their grades to the temperature of all foods and liquids that enter their bloodstream—everything has to be room temperature. Much to my dismay, I've seen this woman heat up orange juice. She is an enemy of ice, and therefore—in my opinion—an enemy of the state.

The first half of the week was spent finding opportunities for me and my two older nephews, ages thirteen and sixteen, to sneak out of the house to swim in caves or jump off of cliffs, where their mother couldn't find us. Advance work was necessary to introduce the boys to fun. If Olga sees anything adjacent to danger—which in her mind could be an open body of water, a lap pool, or a can opener—she will insert herself and cancel the fun. One must always be one step ahead of her. In the beginning of the trip, I held high hopes for the adventures I would take the boys on. By the end of the week, I was beaten down, having given up on the hope of a meaningful relationship with my nephews until they graduated from high school and became legal.

"Can you believe how annoying Olga and Glen are with the kids?" I asked Gaby.

"It's pretty unreasonable," she agreed.

"I mean, how much sunblock can you put on someone before it stops working?"

"I'm surprised she doesn't put it in their mouths," Gaby said, handing me a plate of *jamón* to put on the table. "I've never seen anything like it."

My aunt doesn't say a lot, and it's a nice quality in a person, but "nice" isn't the word anyone would use to describe Gaby. Every time she sees me, she shakes her head, almost as if she can't believe what I've gotten away with in life. When I moved to Los Angeles at nineteen and lived on her sofa, she told me if I wanted to be in the entertainment industry, I had better drop some weight.

I have retold this story for years to friends and family alike, while Gaby has consistently denied it ever happened, ridiculing my flair for the dramatic and propensity for exaggeration. I was finally vindicated when Molly found some old home videos from that time in which you can actually hear Gaby saying on camera that if I wanted to make it in Hollywood I had better drop some weight. Molly knows my memory has a solid track record, and when she found the evidence to support what I had been claiming for twenty years, she made sure the whole family watched the footage together in order to clear my good name. In the video, you can see my face turn bright red. Even I felt bad for me. Gaby must have felt like Hitler in that moment, but ever since then we've had a better understanding of each other.

Gaby is Molly's mother, and my mother's sister, and in exchange for the living accommodations I was provided at nineteen, I was required to drive Molly and her eight brothers and sisters to school each morning at seven o'clock. This is when I discovered that I never wanted children. I wasn't upset by the realization that I wasn't cut out for motherhood. I was only upset that I hadn't thought of it sooner.

. . .

By the end of our family vacation week in Spain, I stopped going to meals with my brother and his family. If I woke up and heard anyone speaking Russian, I'd go downstairs for my medication.

"I can't take any more kids or any more Russians," I told Gaby, popping a doggy Xanax. "I'm going to take a nap."

"You just woke up," she told me.

"Who's that person?" I asked Molly, gesturing to the front balcony, where a woman and my sister-in-law were sitting.

"That's Olga's Russian friend who stopped by last night when you came down from your bedroom in your bra and underwear to get another Xanax."

"So, I've already met her?"

"Well, she met you, but I wouldn't say that you met her."

That's how I felt about my trip to Formentera—it met me, but I didn't meet it.

. . .

On our return flight, Chunk and I had the two seats next to each other with the option of putting the partition up or down. We chose down.

Once Chunk and I were both comfortably settled in and each watching our respective movies, I popped a Xanax and then realized there was none left for Chunk. I didn't want to knock myself out with Chunk awake, so I took one of my weaker sleeping pills I had brought and tried to get him to swallow it. After failing to get it down his throat for the third time, I opened the capsule and emptied it into about two ounces of water and Chunk drank it down.

I had been using Sonata ever since I learned how terrible Xanax was for your brain: the memory loss, the irritability the next day, the fact that it makes you dumb. I justified abusing it that week because of the Russian interference in my summer vacation. Right before I passed out, I wrapped Chunk's leash around my waist and tucked it into the back of my jeans.

Hours later, a flight attendant shook me awake and told me that my dog was loose and running around the first-class cabin. The simple task of standing up suddenly became incredibly difficult to accomplish, as I was lying on my side and had one leg swung over Chunk's seat, where his body had been. My body was confusing me, as was the situation. I could hear Chunk's panting, which sounded almost maniacal. I stumbled through the first-class cabin in a fugue state, scared by the heavy throat-clearing, coughing sounds I was hearing—and at one point during all the confusion, I called out Brandon's name.

When I found Chunk, he was licking the bathroom door with no leash in sight. I grabbed him by the collar and ushered him back to our double pod, where I had to force him to get back up on the seat. His tongue was almost touching the floor and there was foam on either side of his mouth. He looked like he had just snorted an eight ball.

I had never seen Chunk in that state before. I grabbed one of those miniature bottles of room temperature water they give you on planes, but thought Chunk would appreciate something more refreshing—like a Fresca—and then bounced back to reality and recognized I was talking about a dog who was on the verge of swallowing his own tongue. I started by pouring the water into the tiny plastic lid, but after Chunk almost swallowed that, I made a cup out of my hand and started pouring the water in there. When that didn't suffice, I gave up and just started pouring the water directly into his mouth. He wouldn't sit still and kept yanking his head around to get out, but I held him down, trying to get a handle on the situation. The shame that enveloped my double pod took the shape of two blankets I converted into a fort covering the tops of our seats in an effort to prevent the two of us from causing any more of a scene.

"Can I get some more water bottles and a bowl?" I whispered, peeking out from under the covers.

"I don't work here," the passenger across the aisle said, as she sat back down in her assigned seat. The procuring of water became a tricky endeavor, as I couldn't leave Chunk to his own devices and I couldn't find his leash. I looked around for the call button, which I generally try to avoid using because of how rude it seems. I also made a mental note of possibly installing that option when I got home to Bel-Air. Brandon would love a bell.

When I stood up to press the button above my head, Chunk made a run for it. I dove over my seat, grabbing his tail. I hit the floor face-first and felt a sharp burn around my stomach. I discovered that Chunk's leash was wrapped around my waist, under my shirt. In my delirium, instead of fastening the clip of the leash to Chunk's collar, I had clipped it to one of the belt loops on my jeans.

"Can we please get him an entrée?" I asked the flight attendant from the floor, when she headed over to me with three large bottles of water.

When the flight attendant looked at me sideways, I told her I was pregnant. Once I got Chunk nicely settled with his second gallon of water and a bowl, I looked at the map in front of my seat, which told me there were six hours left of our flight to Los Angeles.

When the flight attendant arrived with a Salisbury steak and some other gross side dishes, I took out my tray table to play the part of being the passenger who would be eating it. To cement my credibility, I asked her for a glass of red wine and some bread options. I went through the motions of taking out the silverware and cutting off a piece of the steak on the tray, and once the flight attendant was far enough away, I handed it to Chunk. By the time she returned, the entire tray was facedown on Chunk's side of the seat, with food splattered everywhere, while I was wrestling him to get the entire slab of uncut meat out of his mouth. She didn't even bother stopping; she just turned around and took the red wine and bread with her.

There was water, food, and dog hair everywhere. I fastened Chunk's leash to his collar and placed the handle grip around my ankle. It was time to get real. I recovered the blankets and reinstalled our fort until I could get the situation under control.

I rang the call button once more and ordered a double espresso.

"Would you like one or two?" she asked, eyeing Chunk.

. . .

A week earlier, Chunk had been too dignified to lie on his back to get his belly rubbed. He would rather be caught shoplifting than lie in such a submissive position. It was too ungentlemanly. Chunk even knew it was wrong to get a hard-on. He turned his back when he had to go number two. He was august. He was esteemed.

And now here we were—on a flight where Chunk had lost his last shred of dignity because his delinquent mother force-fed him a human sleeping pill.

I could see the headlines now: "Chelsea Handler Kills Dog on Flight from Spain." PETA would have a field day with this.

Once Chunk was hydrated, his breathing slowed and

he started to calm down, and then, finally—exhausted from the emotional turmoil—he fell asleep. In between checking his pulse and cleaning up the food and dog hair that was splattered all over our area, I became aware of a soreness on my back and abdomen. When I lifted my shirt, I discovered several rope burns.

I quickly realized that I had to start planning for the very real possibility that Chunk might shit his pants on this flight. I had my very aromatic grapefruit hand lotion in the toiletry bag inside my purse, so the plan I devised was to scoop up any fecal matter with the Maxi Pad–grade pillowcase, douse it with the hand lotion to cover the smell, and then flush it down the toilet. I had empty water bottles lined up and ready to place over Chunk's penis in case he decided to pee. I didn't know the protocol for when your dog shits on a plane. Would we be arrested upon landing? *Surely, this can't be a felony.*

. . .

Not only did Chunk not die on the flight, he didn't urinate or take a shadoobie. He waited the entire haul through customs, where the officer greeted the two of us with a "Welcome home, Chunk" and then asked me for my passport. This kind of shit happened with Chunk all the time. Chunk was a national treasure, and I was his plus-one. He'd get recognized on the streets when my houseman Oscar would take him for his morning walks, and even when he would be catching a breeze in the backseat of my car on our way to work. You'd hear other drivers at stoplights say, "Look, that's Chunk," and he'd wag his tail and smile. People would stop us and ask me to take pictures of them with Chunk. He probably went through life assuming getting recognized daily happened to all dogs.

By the time I got home, I looked like the one who should have been on a leash through customs. I was using my eyeshades as a scrunchie, I was covered in dog hair and food stains, and I was bleeding from one arm. I looked like a streetwalker.

Later, when I told my vet what had happened, he informed me that giving a dog a sleeping aid when they're in a state of agitation will just prolong that state of agitation. I told my vet that I was in a constant state of agitation, and whenever I took a sleeping pill, it worked. I didn't mention to the doctor that I had prescribed my own medication for Chunk, or that I had pilfered his on my family vacation.

I avoided eye contact with Chunk for days after we got back from Spain. He knew I was the culprit in this situation, and I had absolutely no defense. For fear of being accused of Munchausen syndrome by proxy, I stopped giving Chunk his CBD oil too. I knew I had overstepped, and it was time to get my dog clean.

"Wouldn't you just kill to know what Chunk is thinking?" Molly asked me one day over oysters I had shucked earlier that afternoon.

"Not anymore," I told her. "That's a slippery slope."

My brother Glen once told me the reason your first-born is so special is because they're the one that makes you a parent. That's how I felt about Chunk. He made me a mother. A delinquent, useless one—but a mother nonetheless.

OH,
MOTHER

The first thing my mother did when she woke up was take a nap. She took on average two naps per day and was in bed for the night no later than nine P.M. Our whole family has the sleep gene, and although I can easily get into bed for the night at 7:30 P.M., I have an aversion to taking unmedicated naps. The last time I fell asleep during the day was after a marijuana facial, when I came home in a stupor and passed out for four hours—at eleven o'clock in the morning. I was high for three days after that and haven't felt entirely right since.

My mother was a lah-dee-dah-dee-dah kind of person. She would go about her day humming "Lah-dee-dah-dee-dah-dee-dah." She wasn't unintelligent; she was just the kind of person who was interested in having a pleasant, ho-hum kind of day. She would never insert herself into anything adjacent to conflict. She wasn't really very good at follow-through, so she had lots of different half-completed projects at home that would usually involve some sort of jury-rigged, repurposed household item that didn't quite cut it, like a bedsheet that was converted into a window shade and embellished with a makeshift border she'd knitted that afternoon. When the project was interrupted by a nap, it was likely to be abandoned.

Our house looked a lot like Sesame Street—the main distinction being it was unsafe for children. She always wanted change. She wanted newness. She got it mostly by experimenting with casseroles and rearranging furniture. I'd come home one day only to stub my toe on a bunch of cinder blocks that had been placed under my bed as my new "bed frame," because my mom had decided my actual metal bed frame looked better in the backyard as an enclosure for our dog, Mutley. She would have knit something for that too—crafting it to look like a questionable art installation. She wasn't crazy. She didn't drink or take drugs. She was a homemaker, and sometimes her ideas were out of left field . . . or in left field . . . many just belonged somewhere in a field.

My mother could sew, knit, plant a garden, and cook. She made the thickest, creamiest macaroni and cheese and the richest, gooiest brownies—both of which were out of a box. But she always made home and food feel better. She could cook pretty much anything, but if you ever asked her for a recipe, she'd just say, "Put a little of this, and a little of that . . . lah-dee-dah-dee-dah-dee-dah." There was nothing exacting about her, ever. Everything with her was always very vague.

She could build pretty much anything too—a deck, a doghouse; she even once built a stone retaining wall in our backyard. She could probably have built a car. It would have broken down eventually, but she definitely could have gotten something going.

The women in our family are on the masculine side, to say the least. We are not girly, we are not wearing dresses, and most of us are not getting laid. My mom had two sisters, and between the three of them they had nine daughters, and somehow, my mom was the most feminine of us all. Her name was Rita, but I called her Chunk.

When I think of her, the first image that comes to mind is of her standing upstairs, leaning over the balcony that looked down over our living room on Martha's Vineyard, eating whatever sandwich she had made to lull her to sleep that night, watching us play board games at the kitchen table. She liked hearing us before she went to sleep. She wanted to listen to us eating and drinking and laughing and playing Balderdash, but she never played, even though my dad always did. She was never a participant. She was always in the background—but always front and center.

My mom knew that her kids needed her after Chet died, and she came back to us way sooner than my dad did. Whereas my dad was incapable of grieving and finding joy at the same time, my mother instinctively managed to do both.

• • •

I was thirty-one years old and in London for my very first book tour, when my cellphone rang in the middle of the night. It was my sister Simone.

"You should come home. Mom isn't doing well."

I knew this call was coming. I knew when I flew to London that my mother was going to interrupt things.

Two months earlier, I was sitting in my parents' living room when Simone came down the stairs from their bedroom, slumped down on the sofa, put her head in her hands, and sobbed. It was eerily reminiscent of when my dad had lost his composure after Chet died. I had never seen Simone be weak. If I had, I didn't remember it. She wouldn't have been weak in front of me, since she had always been a mother figure to me.

My sister gets along with every person she meets. Everyone loves Simone. She's a conflict avoider, a passive, popular, easygoing sorority president—she's eminently reasonable.

Is she really surprised by this outcome? I thought, sitting next to her on the couch. This was my mother's third bout of cancer . . . *What did Simone think was going to happen?* I didn't say those things to my sister. I felt bad for her. I also felt guilty that I wasn't dreading my mother's death as she was—I just wanted to get it over with. My mom had been fighting cancer for so many years—in and out of chemo and radiation, bald, not bald, always a little sick. She never complained, and when she started sleeping more hours a day than she was awake, and could eat only applesauce for weeks at a time, it seemed the writing was on the wall.

After all, everything had been leading up to this—the glue of the family was becoming unglued because she was tired of the chaos. She was tired of living through my father's never-ending lawsuits—his financial unevenness. Being married to my father would have given anyone cancer. My mom was tired of fighting, and she was enervated. Her idea of heaven was dreaming about life while she slept, so in her mind, I'm sure, she was actually looking forward to being able to watch all of us without having to participate. In the afterlife, she would have a front-row seat to all of our lives, but from a higher perch and without the need to get dressed in something other than a housedress. She was worn-out.

I didn't feel sad that my mom was going to die; I felt sad that no one in my family seemed prepared for it. When I saw my sisters suffering at the prospect of her leaving, I felt like they hadn't learned their lesson the last time. There was my lack of empathy again. Never understanding that other people may be receiving things differently.

That's okay, I told myself. I didn't need my sisters to be fighters. *I have enough spinach for all of us.*

Death.

This, I know how to do.

Move over, everyone.

. . .

I went straight to the hospital when I flew in from London, where I found my brother Glen and my dad sitting in a hospital room like two useless cartoon characters, with my mother lying there half-unconscious, weak, and listless— with a fucking roommate who had visitors who reeked of cigarettes. My mom hated cigarettes.

I may as well have seen a priest raping a child. The hell

I raised at the nurses' station was so disruptive and hair-raising that there were people who didn't come back to work the next day—or maybe ever.

I remember Glen grabbing me by the shoulders in the hallway, telling me I had to calm down, and a nurse threatening to remove me from the hospital if I didn't, and me telling her that she would be the one getting removed. The next thing I remember was wheeling my mother's hospital bed into the hallway while I instructed my father and Glen to grab onto any machines that were attached to her body and to follow my lead.

For the record, I would like to state that never in the history of humankind has a woman been told to calm down and then calmed down. We don't like that.

Once we got my mom situated in a private room down the hall, I got into bed next to her. She put her hand in mine and said in the thirstiest of sounds, "Please help me die."

This was the opportunity to show my mother that she could depend on me, that for all the times I fucked up and for all the grief I caused her by never listening to anything either of my parents ever said and constantly getting into trouble in and out of school—that for her last wish, I was listening and I would show up. I was going to prove that she wasn't wrong about me. That finally she could depend on me. Those were my marching orders, and I wasn't going to leave until I had fulfilled her request. It didn't occur to me that she may have said that to all my siblings, looking for anyone to bite.

She spent the next week in her private room, surrounded by her children. I slept on the bed next to her every night. Sometimes, in the morning, I'd leave her side after her first dose of morphine—when she would drift away again—to go to the cafeteria for some eggs, and then be sick at myself for having an appetite. I would remind myself that I needed to stay strong to help my mother die. I was in full-on Joan of Arc mode, and I was not going to make dying a problem for my mother. I hadn't been so laser-focused on anything in my life, ever.

The one time I left her to go home and take a shower, I came back to find her covered in her own vomit, most of it pooled in her newly cavernous collarbones—like two gravy boats. My father was sitting with all four corners of the newspaper facing her—as if he were in his own living room—and hadn't even noticed. He was proving to be as useless as a gorilla underwater, and took up about the same amount of space. I never left her alone with the nurses—or my father—again.

In between bouts of unconsciousness, she would spring to life and utter these fully formed sentences that would render you speechless.

"Once I'm gone, you're going to find out what a piece of work your father is, and I will be laughing at you from heaven," she'd say. Then she'd turn her head, close her eyes, and drift off again, and I'd be left sitting there, looking at my clueless father reading the op-ed page.

I remember looking at her, wondering how she could be so sharp and so with it, while also floating in and out of consciousness. I learned that people have moments of clarity when they're dying, called "terminal lucidity." Or that they'll sometimes seem like they're getting better only to fall further the next day, kind of like a death rally.

"You don't know your own strength," she said to me one afternoon, squeezing my hand. "Please use it for something good. I know you are going to have a big life, but don't forget about your brothers and sisters. And promise me you'll always wear your seatbelt."

"Get a spoon," she said to me with her eyes closed, the day I was cleaning the vomit out of her collarbones. Then she opened her eyes and said, "Promise me you'll take care of Roy and Shana."

I had no idea my mom thought I was capable of taking care of anyone, but she empowered me to think that I was, thus creating the certainty that I would be able to do so.

One day she brushed my cheek with the back of her hand and said, "He needs to let me go."

I looked at my father, who was sitting five feet away—in his diurnal spot, always with the newspaper, this time with a half-eaten Egg McMuffin sitting on his knee. The fact that he hadn't inhaled it in one fell swoop meant that he must have had another meal on the way over.

"You need to say goodbye to Mom," I told him. "She needs you to let her go."

He peeked over the top of the newspaper to make sure he'd heard what he thought he heard.

"Keep her alive, no matter what. She can be on life support." I got up and ripped the paper down the middle, with my hands trembling. It was dramatic, but my mom deserved drama. She had put up with too much shit from both me and my father for way too long. If there was ever a time she would accept a fuss being made over her, it was in her death—and by one or both of the people that caused her the most grief.

"Keep her alive, no matter what?" I was standing in his face and his eyes widened. "Do you know how selfish that is?"

"I've got to go show a car," he announced, bracing himself to get up from the chair he was smothering. My father never sat in a chair. He assaulted it, and the chair was seldom the same.

"A car?"

"Yeah, a guy called me about a car. He's in West Orange."

That was when I knew my father wasn't equipped to deal with what was happening. Death had happened once, and he didn't like the way that turned out, so it wasn't going to happen again. I thought about how sad men are. How little they know about helping women with their feelings. I realize it's not entirely their fault, because they're wired differently and they've been raised for thousands of years to act like this, but it's still hard when you see it up close and personal—especially when it's your own father.

"Okay," I told him. "Go do that. Mom and I will probably just go waterskiing."

. . .

There were supposed to be four hours between drips of morphine, but when she was uncomfortable, I would summon the nurse, who would come in and reiterate to me that it had been only two hours since her last dose.

"Do you have a fucking mother?" I wailed. I hadn't left the hospital for five days and was starting to look like Gary Busey.

The nurses had stopped communicating with me soon after I arrived, and I can't blame them, but a four-hour pain-medication protocol when someone is clearly dying is a set of rules that needs to be changed. We should be allowed to help one another die. We shouldn't have to scream and yell and throw tantrums, but obviously in the interim, I am and will always be a person willing to take on that role. There are things you can do for other people that you can never do for yourself.

Whenever I have trouble standing up for myself (*it's happened*), I think about whether I would tolerate the situation if it were happening to one of my sisters, mother, daughter, or niece. If it's not acceptable for them, it's not acceptable for me. I was born with a torch in my hand, and I haven't always used it so judiciously, but this was an instance where I needed to protect my mother—because she didn't have the strength to protect herself. She never did. She was never like that. She was shy, demure, soft-spoken, sweet, mushy, and full of womb-like feelings. She was always there for a hug or a cuddle, but I couldn't ask her for advice. She had been sidelined by my father, and the way I saw things, she had very little say in anything. If my father hadn't really loved her, it could have been a disaster.

"Just answer the question!" I screamed at the nurse after she told me it had been only two hours since her last morphine. "Do you have a mother?"

The nurse came over and upped my mom's morphine,

and then put her hand on top of my mother's. I saw my mom's hand tighten around the nurse's. "Can you imagine having a daughter like this one?" she said.

When we were told it would only be a matter of days, we decided to transfer her to a hospice, where they would give her as much morphine as she wanted and stop trying to force-feed her. I rode in the ambulance with her head in my hands, because every time we made a turn, it felt like a coconut falling from a tree.

Once she was in hospice, none of us left again until she died. Well, my father did, because he, of course, needed to eat something in order to re-clog his arteries every few hours.

The night before my mother died, the five of us were sleeping on cots in her room. Glen and I were sleeping on one side, while Shana and Roy were on the other side of the room next to each other. Simone was sitting up in a chair.

"Chelsea," Glen whispered. "How long do you think Shana and Roy have been sleeping together?"

"Seriously, Glen," Simone muttered from across the room.

That's what death is like, though. You can't only cry for two weeks straight. You cry, and then you get tired of crying, and someone says something, and then you're all laughing, and then it feels bad to be laughing, but it also feels so good. Without the laughter, we'd all be dying too.

The day my mother died, we were all in the room with her. Her body got cold, and Shana, being a nurse, told us what was happening. My mom was starting to turn blue, but she was always a little blue. She had an alabaster complexion. We sat and held hands and cried together, until my father interrupted us.

"We're going to need to discuss the funeral details," he announced to the room with my mother's still-warm body. "She's got to be buried in the plot next to Chet, so it's going to have to be a Jewish funeral."

"But she's Mormon," Shana blurted. Shana was Mormon too. She had converted to Mormonism years earlier with the help of my mother. After Chet died, my mom threw in the towel on Judaism and got back to her Mormon roots. When Shana was a freshman in college at the University of Delaware, my parents got a call that she was very sick and they drove to go pick her up. After weeks of testing, they diagnosed her with lupus. They say that when there is a death in a family, it's not uncommon for family members to develop diseases in the years following. Who knows if this is true, but five years later, Shana got lupus and then my mom got cancer. After Shana got sick, she turned to Mormonism. The Jews in our family were dropping like hot potatoes.

"Jewish cemeteries won't allow non-Jews to be buried there," Glen informed us. "We have to have a fake Jewish funeral."

"What about all of her friends from church?" Shana asked.

"They're just going to have to pretend she's Jewish, for the funeral," Glen said, matter-of-factly—as if this is what all families do when there's a death, have a fake funeral. It seemed like Glen had already sorted this out with my father and was breaking the news to the rest of us.

"What if they find out she isn't Jewish? What about her bishop or friends from church who want to say something about her?" Shana asked. "They all know she's not Jewish."

"They're not allowed," my dad told her. "They can go do their own thing."

"You know, like have a service at a local supermarket," Glen told Shana. Glen can be an asshole in these instances. He doesn't mean to be, but he's just another man who doesn't know how to handle women when they are in crisis.

My dad announced that he needed us to get him something to wear for the funeral—"None of my nice suits fit anymore"—and then he walked out of the room.

Glen's eyes rolled into the back of his head. "I wonder why."

"Dad doesn't know that Mom baptized Chet," Shana said quietly.

"Are you serious?" Simone asked, appalled.

"Yes," Shana declared.

"Mom baptized Chet?" I asked. Just another fucking thing that no one in my family ever bothered to tell me.

"So, now we have two non-Jews that will be buried in a Jewish cemetery," Glen declared, smiling. "Sounds like there's an odd man out."

"Can we just baptize Dad after he dies, and then they can all be buried together?" Roy asked.

"That's a great idea, Roy," Glen told him. "That ought to fix everything."

"Does being baptized negate your Judaism?" I asked.

"Not if you're dead when they baptize you," Glen whispered, as he gently kissed my mother on her forehead. It was a perfect Glen moment—tender, but dripping with sarcasm.

"Actually, in the Book of Mormon . . ." Shana started, and I had to interrupt her.

"Please don't with the Mormon stuff right now. I just can't."

"She'd want to be next to Chet," Simone said.

"Yeah, but would she want to be next to Dad?" Glen asked.

We sat in silence for a few minutes trying to make sense of what was about to take place. Then Roy—who had had a bar mitzvah thirty years earlier, and never converted—asked, "Am I Mormon too?"

These are the times when you think no family is as fucked-up as your own, and that no one on earth has been through anything close to what you've been through.

. . .

We all dealt with Chet in our own way, and now it was time for us to split up and deal with our mom dying, individually. But we didn't. We stuck together this time—perhaps from knowing the mistake we made last time.

Shana and I drove to the Short Hills mall to pick out something for her to wear. Shana has extremely short legs and two bricks for feet. Buying clothes for her is and always will be confounding. The looks of the saleswomen at Saks and Nordstrom are always entertaining to behold—if you like diplomacy mixed with a healthy dose of bewilderment.

While we were shopping, I tried to convince her that an

A-line skirt was just what she needed to meet someone romantically at our mother's funeral. She reminded me that she was already married with a baby. I got her to laugh and she got me to laugh because that is what sisters do for each other in the depths of their despair—they cry, laugh, sing, fight, and then go see a movie, in that order.

My sister and I buoyed each other that day. I thought my mom would be proud of how we guided each other through this death storm. Then we got back to Shana's house, and when I came upstairs from putting our bags away, I found her standing in the rain on her back porch, crying inconsolably. Her husband was standing in the kitchen staring at her, not knowing what to do. Who would know what to do? Sisters. Only a sister knows how to comfort a sister. Period. End of story. Men can give us a hug or pat us on the back, but only a girl will get another girl off her feet to face the rain. That is the definition of sisters. There exists between us an ineffable understanding. We don't have to ask why or how or when. We just go in.

Sometimes, I'm there. Sometimes, Shana is there. Sometimes, Simone is there. One of us is always there. We've all been one another's mother at some point.

It hurt to see Shana in so much pain, and I felt guilty that my pain didn't cut as deep. She was close to my mother in a way that I never was. She was more dependent and more loving, and they were more alike. My sister would have taken advice from my mother. Both were reserved, sweet, and Mormon together. I never appreciated or respected that.

When my sister converted to Mormonism after Chet

died, it felt like one more strike against her. Religion was of no interest to me, and when I read the Book of Mormon at my mother's behest, I came away even more embarrassed for both of them. It all bored me to no end. Religion wasn't going to ever be my jam, and I didn't appreciate trying to be converted in the privacy of my own home. It all felt so sanctimonious. The notion that accepting Jesus Christ as your savior absolved you of all wrongdoing of any scale felt like a crock of shit.

Shana and my mom had a special bond, and in that moment, I felt my sister's pain way worse than any pain I had myself. I knew I'd be fine. I wondered how long it would take her to be fine. *She's got children; she'll get better faster because of them.* I reminded myself that a parent dying is more commonplace than a child dying; therefore, Shana would have to pull herself together at some point. People's parents die all the time. This wouldn't be like last time.

• • •

I remember every finger on my mother's hand and her inveterately chipped nail polish. She would never have gotten a proper manicure or pedicure. My mom had a low tolerance for that kind of frilly stuff. She liked to grow her nails long and paint them herself, but it was always a crapshoot. Her fingers were chubby but somehow elegant. She was chubby and elegant too. I could pick her hands out of a lineup of a thousand.

She was gracious and dignified, two qualities I am in short supply of. My grace is grit, and my dignity is outrage. She would cover her mouth when she laughed, and she hated being photographed—she was from that era. I always wanted my mom to smile big. I wanted that for her. She probably didn't care about it, but I wanted her to be freer. I wanted her to throw caution to the wind, not be so ladylike, to be a little bit bawdy and crass—I wanted her to be more like me.

She was nothing like me. My mother would have probably hated me, had I not been her daughter. She was warm and fuzzy and chunky with lots of side pockets of meat to grab onto, which always made me feel like I was home. It's why I love meaty pets and meaty babies and meaty people. My mom wanted the best for her kids, but she and I both knew that she was probably not the person who would be providing it. She never wanted you to be sad—or to cry. She had a ton of compassion. And empathy in spades. She always wanted everyone to be happy, to feel better. She was soft with her touch, and always had her arms open for anyone who needed comfort.

She worried about Shana and Roy. She always told me she never worried about me. She never held any of my past behavior against me; she never passed judgment—she was always ready with new unconditional love. She was my mother—the person who would love me more perfectly than anyone else ever would and never asked for much in return. When my dad and I went through our rough years, she did whatever she could to make the situation better for me. She knew my father was an asshole. She knew I was one too, and with two assholes in such close proximity, I'm sure she wondered what it was about her personality that drew those types of people to her.

. . .

"It takes an asshole to make an asshole. You got it from your father," she told me after I told her I was pregnant at sixteen and planning to move to Niagara Falls, where I could raise my baby in peace. When my mom yelled at you it was hard to take her seriously—it was almost like she had peanut butter in her mouth. Hearing my mother curse always put a smile on my face, even when things were bad. She didn't do it often, but when she did it, you looked up.

"You're not having a baby. You'll ruin your life. I'll let you do almost anything else, but I will not let you bring a child into this world—not while you're still acting like one. You have no idea what that responsibility is like."

"Well, it doesn't seem that hard," I told her. "You can just sleep all the time and never show up to anything."

I was terrible as a teenager. I always had a knee-jerk re-action to things I didn't like hearing. I put my mother through hell, but she never gave up on me, and she never stopped loving me. She always told me she knew I would turn out okay, and that I just needed my independence, and that once I was an adult, I would shake myself out. Maybe that was another thing she made true, simply by saying it.

When my father and I used to go to war, he would yell at me and throw his hands up and say, "She's not right! Something is wrong with her!"

My mom would tell him not to talk about me like that—that I was in pain and I needed to get it out of my system. I overheard her say that to him once while they were arguing about me. I thought then about how out of focus that seemed. *It has nothing to do with pain—I just want a different family.* I know now that it had everything to do with pain, and that what I wanted was my family back in one piece. If I took control of making my family dysfunctional, then I would never have to mourn anyone again.

• • •

My best friend from high school told me many years later that my mom was the first person to tell her she loved her. I couldn't believe that. I could believe my mom did something like that, but I also couldn't believe her own parents had never told her they loved her. Another broad reminder that your experience isn't like everyone else's. I never felt unloved. I felt disappointed, and abandoned, but I never felt like I wasn't loved.

"No one had ever told me that before," my friend said. "Your mom told me she loved me and that I was lovable. She just somehow knew I needed to hear that."

• • •

The day of the funeral, I headed upstairs to my mom's medicine cabinet. Roy was already standing there looking through the options. "What do we got?" I asked.

"Valium, Norco?" he said.

"That's like Vicodin."

"Codeine?"

"That's good."

"Percocet?"

"That's pretty strong. Give me the Percocet and you take the rest. By the way, all of these things make you constipated," I told him.

Roy pursed his lips to indicate he had bigger problems at the moment, but I knew, as a pharmacological intuit, I had the duty to inform him of all pertinent side effects. I had been prescribing drugs to people for years, and I knew the ethical guidelines that go with said profession. I can tell by someone's weight, body type, personality, and mood what the right dosage for them will be. I'd known my brother my whole life. He needed a Vicodin.

My dad walked out of the closet he shared with my mom wearing a pair of suspenders strapped to a pair of khakis and a shirt that he couldn't button all the way. He looked like a giant baby.

"I don't think so, buddy," I told him.

"Nothing fits," he declared.

"Neither does what you're wearing."

"What are you two doing in there?" he asked, cocking his head to one side, playfully. "Careful with that stuff. It's strong."

Roy elbowed me, like we were twelve. Once I was an adult, I knew I always had the upper hand with my father, simply by virtue of telling the truth.

"It's Percocet," I told him. "Do you want one?"

"No, I don't touch the stuff. But you should take two. I don't want you to have another one of your hysterical hospital episodes at the funeral."

I wondered if my father was relieved that my mother was dead. I remember looking at him in those suspenders with his giant belly protruding, thinking, *Why on earth did*

I bother fighting so hard to keep you alive, when my mother was the one worth fighting for? Then I thought about my mother watching us from where she believed she was going, and thought, *She's already laughing at us,* and then I was laughing, and then my father, and then Roy.

My father's plan for my mother's funeral was exactly the kind of hijinks we'd all learned to expect from him. The funeral was a long afternoon of avoiding eye contact with anyone Mormon. This was the epitome of our family. We couldn't even get death right.

After my mom died, my dad acted like my sisters and I were just going to pick up where she left off, as if there had been some indication that we had any of her talent or gift for homemaking. He simply presumed that because we were related to my mother, we could all make a casserole out of matzoh. My sisters would complain about him showing up at their houses demanding a fresh-cooked meal. Nothing is more annoying than someone who can't cook pretending they can, and none of us can cook, but somehow during that time, my father must have convinced Simone that she had the gift. She got on this recipe kick for a while—because my father was tricking her into making food for him—and she'd talk about cooking as if she had just somehow magically inherited my mother's culinary skills. She acted like she was the first person who ever roasted a chicken with peaches. Hopefully, the last.

· · ·

I grew up with people always telling me that I looked like my mother. When I was a teenager, my mother was old and chubby in my eyes—I loved her, but I didn't want to look like her. Now that she's gone, I always look for myself in pictures of her. I want to resemble her now. Probably the same way parents look for themselves in their children. I guess it's all about whoever is on the other side of the looking glass. Now I want to look like my mother, and—guess what—now that I'm older, I do.

My mom died a day before I was supposed to start production on my very first TV show, *The Chelsea Handler Show*. This was a short-lived venture that turned into *Chelsea Lately*.

While her life was ending, mine felt like it was finally starting to make sense. I had been doing stand-up for years, I had published my first book, and my future had begun. New Jersey represented the past. My life was in Los Angeles now. I wanted the past to be over and the rest of my life to begin.

Keep moving. Keep doing. Keep going.

Weirdly, the relationship between my mother and me strengthened after she died. It was then that I felt her looking over me and after me, way more than what I felt when she was on earth.

Every day before I went onstage for *Chelsea Lately*, I would stand backstage and look up and imagine this warm, glowing light.

Whenever I got nervous, I would always think of my mother. I'd look up, and welcome her light, and ask her to watch over me, and help me shine. It used to happen when I was performing, but now it happens mostly when I'm skiing, because that is where I'm willing to take almost any risk to get better. When I ski, I sometimes feel my mother's hand on my shoulder. Sometimes it's Chet's hand I feel.

Slow down, I'll hear, when I'm gunning down a mountain out of control. *Cool it*, one of them will say, and sometimes I do. I listen to my mother more now than I ever did when she was standing in front of me.

She knew I was reliable before I did. She knew about my strength before I did. She knew my sister needed extra love, and she knew my father was one big hot mess that she needed to try to shield us from—protecting us in the best way she could. She knew a lot more than I ever gave her credit for knowing. Her strength was quiet. Her determination wasn't loud or ugly—it was refined. I never knew determination could be quiet. I suppose it depends on who's got it.

My mother died twenty-two years after Chet—the same amount of time he was alive. She had him in her life for twenty-two years, and then she tried for twenty-two years to live without him—and then she gave up. I know now that she did her best.

AYAHUASCA

Whereas siblings tend to police you, cousins are your partners in crime. A cousin is who you go out to breakfast with after a night of debauchery, and who doesn't flinch when you ask the server to put a margarita in your omelet. My sisters would tolerate that behavior, but they wouldn't help me achieve my goal—or try to reason with the server on my behalf. My cousin Molly would.

I would also say that if there's anything better than a cousin or a sister, it's Molly. Technically, she is my cousin, but I think of her as my mother, father, sister, brother, and daughter. We are intertwined. My ugliest is fine with her. I wish I could say the same about her, but her breath in the morning is strong. She knows that although it's not a deal-breaker, she should always have her back toward me when we wake up after a sleepover.

Molly is a producer on all of my projects. Karen is also a producer. Karen started out as my assistant on tour about ten years ago, and then became my personal assistant full-time. When she was ready to move on to a different role, she found Brandon and Tanner to take her place. That's why I call Karen "Bitch." Because it took two men to replace her. Also because she doesn't put up with anyone's shit.

Karen is kind and strong, but she makes you earn her trust. She's from Oklahoma and she's a Christian, and the fact that she supports whatever I do is a testament to the strength of her character. I chose her to come on tour with me initially because she didn't speak very much, and at that time in my life, that's what I was looking for. She also knows how to run a book signing and a comedy tour, and she always lets me find out about people on my own, even though she usually has them pegged months before I do. Like the time I got sick of my therapist (not Dan) and sent Karen in my stead. After her second visit, I asked her if she felt like she was making progress.

"For who?" she asked.

"For *you*," I said.

"I didn't know I was supposed to talk about myself," she said. "I thought I was in there to talk about your problems."

I've learned more from Karen's restraint than she could ever learn from my noise. She disagrees with me on so many topics, yet is the first one to get up and start planning when I say I want to cross the country and talk to Republicans about abortions and guns. We've grown a lot together over the years.

Molly, Karen, and I are a triad.

Molly is the one in charge. Karen supports the decisions Molly or I make, and I do whatever Karen tells me to do.

We have an understanding: They will enable, support, and encourage me, as long as I behave in a loving way toward others and myself. If I behave badly, they are more like disappointed parents whose daughter got suspended from fourth grade for the third time this year.

. . .

The three of us were sitting around my office, brainstorming about a documentary series I was filming for Netflix. We had chosen three topics—marriage, race, and Silicon Valley (and my allergic reaction to technology)—but we needed a fourth.

"I think I should do one about drugs," I said. "It's kind of like my wheelhouse, no?"

"Yes," they both said in unison, as if I asked this question several times a day.

"Do you think Netflix will let you do that?" Molly asked. "Won't that just sound like another one of your boondoggles?"

Molly likes to write down words that I throw around or misuse, look them up, and then use them properly in a sentence directed at me.

"You guys want to do it with me?" I asked them, winking at Molly for her on-point usage of "boondoggle."

"I'm not doing any drugs on camera," Karen said, zipping up her sweatshirt.

"I would," Molly said, "but if we film this, I'll technically be working. I don't think anyone's going to go for that."

"Why not? Chelsea will also be 'working,'" Karen reminded us.

"Yes, but Chelsea's 'work' requires different things from her than ours does from us," Molly said.

. . .

My first choice of drug was mushrooms, my favorite, but that is pretty much illegal everywhere. Someone mentioned ayahuasca. This is the drug that's derived from a plant in South America and brewed into a tea that you drink. More often than not, you shit your pants, vomit, and then have some sort of transcendental experience—in that order. There are some people who actually have mental breakdowns during their experience, but I have always felt that I'm not a candidate for that sort of thing.

"I don't know how I feel about shitting my pants on camera," I told them.

"Why?" Molly asked. "That seems like something you would do."

"They don't *have* to film you actually shitting your pants on camera," Karen reminded us. "And I'm sure you don't *have* to shit your pants. I'm sure production can secure a toilet or a bucket for you. They can't force you to shit your pants like a *baby*."

"But can *we*?" Molly asked Karen, with one eyebrow raised to somewhere between the middle of her forehead and her hairline.

"To do it legally, you'd have to go to South America. It says here, Peru is pretty much the place for that," Karen said, squinting at her computer.

Molly's eyes lit up, and she wiggled her shoulders. "You looooove Peru."

Molly and I had just come back from Peru, where we'd gone after I announced that I was ready to tackle my phobia of snakes. This idea was based simply on the time of day, the amount of marijuana in my system, and my willingness to travel anywhere, for any reason. We were in Santiago, Chile, tagging along on one of my brother Glen's "business trips," when it dawned on me that Peru was basically up the street.

We had gotten some weed off of our sixty-seven-year-old driver in Santiago—who refused to take any money for it, being that selling drugs in Chile is a crime whereas gifting them is not. We were all very stoned and exhausted from walking around the city for hours. For some reason, Glen had dragged us from one corner of the city to the next, as if he owned the place, until finally Molly and I told him to fucking cool it.

"Don't go to Peru, Chelsea," Glen said with a scowl, as we sat in the bar of the Ritz-Carlton in Santiago, catching our breath. "That's going to be a full-blown nightmare for you. There are snakes everywhere."

"Ooooh, this is going to be scary," Molly said as she started looking up flights.

"I have no fear of dying," I proclaimed.

"No one should fear dying, Chelsea. It's going to be glorious," Glen said, smiling longingly.

"*Flying,* Glen. I meant flying, not dying."

"Commercially?"

"She means coach," Molly interjected. "Some of these

smaller planes don't have first class. So the whole plane is coach."

"I'd fly coach if it meant finally conquering my fear of snakes."

"Can you imagine if you had to be a flight attendant, Chelsea?" Glen asked me, smiling and looking off into the distance.

"In coach," Molly added.

"You'd be collecting unemployment." This image delighted him to no end.

"Or in jail," Molly said.

I got up and tried to find some chicken fingers. When I realized they weren't just sitting on a table in the lobby of the Ritz-Carlton, I came back to the bar and asked them what the plan for food was.

"You're not hungry, Chelsea," Glen told me. "We've been eating all day. You're just stoned. Sit down and have a drink, like a normal person."

"We're going to Peru," Molly declared, shimmying her shoulders.

"Well, if you're going to go to Peru, then at least go to Machu Picchu," Glen replied. "At least that has a shred of history."

"No one's even talking to you," I reminded him as I tapped on my Fitbit for an update on steps taken and calories burned.

I had recently ended my show *Chelsea Lately* and had signed a deal with Netflix. I had about six months off, a time I was referring to as my sabbatical.

"Chelsea's taking a semester at sea, Glen. Why can't

you be more supportive?" Molly asked with no expectation of an answer.

Molly is always game for anything, so we ignored Glen and booked some lodge that sat on one of the tributaries of the actual Amazon River, Madre de Dios—or Mother of the Gods—and headed to Peru in search of anacondas.

Not only did we not see any anacondas, we didn't see a single animal. Except piranhas—if those even count as animals. We went on a fishing expedition one day and were expected to jump into the water with the piranhas for some sort of cleansing/pedicure experience, and when everyone in our motorized canoe declined to hop into the river, I decided I would be the one to do it—until Molly announced to everyone that I had my period.

For the record, it was Molly who actually had her period, but she knew full well I was only trying to be brave and that I had no real desire to have my legs nipped at by piranhas simply because it had been suggested as an activity. Instead, our guides all fished the piranhas and then fried them for lunch. Obviously, they were delicious—because anything fried is delicious.

The trip was a quarter past awful. I even had Juan, our guide, take us out in the middle of the night with headlamps on like coal miners to search for anacondas—or any snake, for that matter. He had a machete and everything. I was ready to combat my fears, and I was indefatigable in my efforts, yet we saw nothing. Each activity was more boring than the one before, and the whole experience was tantamount to being at a landlocked Sandals resort. We did see lots of large bugs and went on about six nature walks

My dad and me on Martha's Vineyard. Swimming buddies.

My mom on the deck of the Vineyard house in 1975, a few months after I was born.

Me and Shana on the Vineyard, collecting tennis balls to stuff her bra.

Me and my sister, Simone, with her arm always around me, age three.

Shana holding me in Katama Bay, probably while I was peeing.

Chet and me in our
backyard in New
Jersey in 1979.

Celebrating my dad's birthday, which he always claimed was on Thanksgiving—even though Thanksgiving is on a different day every year.

Shana smoking a pipe to try to fit in with me.

On an Easter egg hunt in Martha's Vineyard, at age six.

Chet's college graduation: Simone, me, Chet, my mom, and my grandmother, the German.

Me at nine years old, hugging our family dog, Mutley, who would become the prototype for all my future dogs.

My aunt Ellen, my father, and me at my brother Roy's bar mitzvah.

My mom and me when I was eight. The year before Chet died.

My brother Glen's graduation from college. The year after Chet died.

My father and me at my bat mitzvah in 1988.

My mom and me at a beauty pageant. I was fifteen.

With Simone at my high school graduation, still with her arm around me.

Me and my parents in Martha's Vineyard in 1996, the summer after I moved to California.

My aunt Gaby, me, Simone, and Molly on our Xanax-fueled family vacation.

Visiting my dad at his old-age home in Pennsylvania.

Me and my sissies in San Francisco.

Shana and me, on our way to an event for our
current governor of New Jersey, Phil Murphy, 2017.

Karen and me on my speaking tour to try to understand conservatives, 2018.

Molly and me
on safari in
South Africa.

Chunk on his outbound flight to Spain.

Chunk at the end of our flight
back to America.

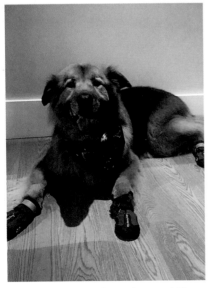

Chunk testing out shoes that would keep
him from flying down the stairwell.

Chunk loved the rain.

Tammy.

Bert, freshly shorn, and Bernice.

This is how Tammy would stiffen whenever I picked her up. She is freshly shorn in this pic because, like Bert, she had some lumps I needed to get a better look at.

The look Bert gives me when Mama leaves the house.

Me trying to pretend my dogs love me.

through miles of woods with large walking sticks, where the most exciting discovery was a butterfly. All the other guests at the lodge were in their mid-seventies, and at some point we realized it was a bird-watching lodge.

. . .

"Ugh, Peru again. That feels like two times too many," I said, lacking any enthusiasm.

"Maybe Peru is calling you back because the ayahuasca will help you conquer your fear of snakes," Molly said, excitedly. "Maybe it's all related. It says here: 'After ayahuasca, people have claimed to get over phobias, quit addictions to drugs and alcohol, and some people end up moving to the jungle and doing it for years.'"

"Well, I'm not going in there with that intention. To shit my pants and then get sober?"

"What about living in the jungle?" Karen asked. "That sounds like an environment you'd thrive in."

"You would never have to deal with Wi-Fi ever again," Molly added. "Or Bluetooth. Or passcodes. Everything could just be J-U-N-G-L-E."

. . .

Anyhoo, a few months later, our production team flew out to Peru with two of my friends in tow. Jenny Mollen and Dan Maurio had agreed to come down to the jungle and take ayahuasca with me. Jenny is pretty much open to anything, and Dan is a small man with a weak constitution. Molly came on the trip as a producer; Karen stayed back because she has a weak stomach—and South America equates to diarrhea in her mind. She's not racist—but she does get diarrhea anytime she leaves the country, whether she's headed north, south, east, or west.

Before you take ayahuasca, it's recommended that you "cleanse." That's usually where my train jumps off the track. I don't like to cleanse in order to do drugs; it feels counterintuitive. They tell you not to eat meat for six weeks or drink alcohol a week prior to your "journey." For the record, I also despise the word "journey." *The Bachelor* ruined that word about ten years ago. A manufactured relationship on a reality show is not a "journey." It's a fake situation—one that has been admitted to time and again by the producers and "contestants." So I skipped the cleanse.

Whatever the cleanse was all about turned out to be true. I took the ayahuasca the first night with two of my friends who had both "cleansed," and both of them intermittently vomited and broke down, while I somehow became more and more sober. I spent the night holding and comforting Jenny, while Dan was moaning on a mat in the corner of the room. I think he had diarrhea, but between his crying and Jenny's crying, it became hard to decipher which noise was coming from what orifice. The situation couldn't have gotten any worse—the final blow being that it was all caught on film and would be airing on Netflix.

Ayahuasca is meant to put things into perspective, and for many, it shines a light on whatever you love most in this world. It turned out Jenny was horrified at how much she loved her husband, while Dan was horrified that he left his pregnant wife and two kids to come to Peru with me, of all people. His contempt for me was apparent on his face and has never quite gone away. We worked together for two years following that trip, and every time I walked into an edit bay where he was running post-production, he would shake his head in disgust.

The next day, the shaman declared that instead of having a full camera crew, we were allowed to bring only one camera. Furthermore, I would have to take double the dosage and not have *any* friends with me—almost like a work camp. Normally, being forced to take psychedelics solo wouldn't sit well with me, but after seeing both Jenny's and Dan's reactions to the ayahuasca, I welcomed the respite of hallucinating alone.

A medium or psychic once told me to think of my mom sending bright, positive beams of light down over me whenever I needed positive energy to calm my nerves or to meditate. I filled my brain with my mother, and everything felt radiant, and warm, and hopeful.

I didn't want to have the same experiences Dan and Jenny had had the night before. I also knew that I wouldn't. If I had been able to control my emotions for this long, and do as many drugs as I have done without ever having a truly bad experience, I knew I would be able to control this experience as well. If it brought up something I couldn't bear to deal with—like Chet—I knew I would be able to shift gears. Then I thought maybe my mother would come through first, but that just seemed too obvious, and besides, with my mother there was no unfinished business.

I could sense something good was going to happen; I knew I had the strength of mind to make something useful come of this. That was my thing—not to leave empty-handed.

I looked at the tiny shaman, in a wifebeater and stone-washed True Religion jeans held up by a giant belt buckle with a Virgin Mary on it, and wondered how he kept any weight on if he was doing ayahuasca every night, shitting his pants. Then I wondered if I would also be lucky enough to lose weight during this experience, and this would be one of those situations I could look back on and say, "After ayahuasca, I was never able to put weight on again."

He instructed me to keep my eyes closed as he chanted a bunch of prayers in a version of Spanish that I assume is only used in the woods, and then he gave me a double shot of what hadn't worked on me the night before. It tasted pretty awful, but if you're a girl trying to look tough in front of your camera crew, you handle it. We went to a different room than we'd been in the night before, much more low-key, with only the shaman, the camerawoman—Nicola—and me. It all felt a little too intimate, but I am often able to do things in front of cameras that I am unable to do when there are no cameras around.

My director and a few others were outside the hut watching on monitors, but the bulk of the crew was all downstairs—presumably drinking.

I was sitting cross-legged on the floor with my eyes closed, and what I experienced first was a light show—a panoply of blues and purples and greens swirling through the air and this undeniable feeling of complete and total equanimity.

Seconds later I was vomiting into the bucket that had

been placed next to me, but even that felt peaceful. It was a pleasant vomit because it just flew out of me—there was no nausea preceding it, and vomiting itself is an art I had perfected in my twenties. Somehow, I did not end up shitting my pants, so once I was done vomiting, I settled into a sort of cruise control, or artificial intelligence—sitting up and looking back and forth at all the images that were speeding by before my eyes.

The blues and purples and greens finally settled on the body of water I spent all of my childhood summers on—Katama Bay. The water was dancing and the laughter was echoing up off of it, up to the sky where I was perched. The laughter was my sister Shana's and mine—as little girls. It was as if I were watching a movie in fast-forward—memories I hadn't thought about in years but were somewhere in my subconscious. Jumping off the dock on Martha's Vineyard, tipping each other over in kayaks, looking for hermit crabs on the beach, all with the buoyancy of little girls' laughter. Nothing ominous. Nothing scary. The laughter was innocent and infectious and uproarious and sweet. That's what it was like—a film I was watching from the sky. You are outside your life, but it is your life. Every memory is real.

There was a dog running along the beach that I had forgotten we had growing up. I saw Shana in the blue-and-white pinstriped bathing suit she wore all the time, throwing him a tennis ball—and then I saw myself as a little girl, running after Shana with my blonde curls bouncing and then grabbing her leg, clumsily pulling her down to the sand with me. Little bellies filled with dancing laughter. I couldn't have been more than three, and I was already tackling my sister.

The dock we used to push each other off of, the little sandy beach we used to play Kadima on. The images were all moving so fast, a phantasmagoria of memories that were all real—memories that were so ingrained in me, that I'd taken for granted and stored in the deep receptacles of my brain. Tears were streaming down my face. I was overwhelmed with love for my sister.

In this moment, I was overcome. I felt the love that Jenny and Dan described—but for my sister, which I hadn't expected. It was this delightfully perfect reminder of what she and I truly are—sisters who've experienced more together than apart. We witnessed how we both have been shaped—that was true intimacy. No self-consciousness, no pretending.

Building sandcastles, digging sand out of our bathing suits, learning to fish, all bundled into the innocence of childhood—before puberty, and boobs, and acne, and boys. How had I forgotten all the times we held hands without even thinking?

All of these images were coupled with this voice in my head telling me that just because my sister wasn't like me didn't mean I had any right to judge her. My sister was perfectly happy being a housewife and living in suburbia; the fact that for some reason that bothered me held absolutely no merit.

My sister and I were two different people, and all she ever wanted was my love. I needed to have more patience and more understanding for her, and I needed to love her harder. *Love her harder.* That's what I was being told. *Be kinder. Be more gentle. Do you know how hard it must be to be your sister?*

Then my thoughts shifted gears to a scene of us on a bunny slope at Vernon Valley Ski Resort. My older brothers and sisters would take us skiing and leave Shana and me in ski school all day. Shana thought that was perfectly fine, but the very notion used to drive me up a wall.

"How could you be okay going up and down the bunny slope on a T-bar while they're out there having the time of their lives, living it up on the slopes?" I asked her, gesturing with my hot chocolate during one of our ski school snacks. "They're making a mockery of us. I think we need to teach them a lesson."

I looked like I was eight, and Shana would have been thirteen, and this would have been our exact dynamic.

Shana wanted to stay put, to follow the rules. I was in an uproar.

"You and I can go skiing on our own. We're too old for ski school. *You're* definitely too old for ski school," I told her, tossing my hot chocolate in the trash.

"They probably just want me to watch you," she told me, half assuring herself.

"Or the other way around," I reminded her. Then I got my mittens and hat, and stormed away from Shana in my ill-fitting ski boots, headed toward anything but the bunny slope.

I remembered the hot chocolate, and I remembered how uncomfortable those boots had been.

Moments later, when I was returned by one of the

mountain employees for not having a proper lift ticket, Shana just shook her head and said, "Do you ever think anything through?"

Watching us together at that age was hilarious. We were both so ridiculous.

Then there was another whoosh of lights that brought me to my sister's living room. This was different because I wasn't in this scene; it was a conversation she had relayed to me months earlier in an email.

My father had come over to her house—this was before we moved him into a facility, before he needed twenty-four-hour care, while he was still a homeowner and the proud driver of the same beat-up gold minivan he had been driving since my mother died, with the same used, empty coffee cups that were in there when she died. My father's idea of a car wash is to drive by one. Why he still needed a minivan and who he was transporting in it were questions none of us wanted the answers to. He would frequently stop by one of my siblings' homes, wearing a diaper that would somehow always manage to leak, forcing them all to dread his visits and put towels down when he came over. Does it get any more undignified? (Not a question.)

Shana had just gotten a call from a man claiming to be my father's son. His story was that my dad got his mother pregnant right before my father met my mother, and that when said woman came to tell my father she was pregnant, my dad told her he was getting married and to back off. The son was interested in my father's medical history for the purpose of his and his children's genetic inheritance.

My sister told our new brother that our dad had a lot of health issues. That he was alive, but in decline.

Our new brother told Shana that, ideally, he'd like to talk to my father, to which she responded, "You're going to be disappointed. He's old, and he's not completely with it. He's a real piece of work."

Shana conveyed all of this to me in an email with a photo of our so-called brother attached. He looked more like my father than any of us.

I remember that the very act of her sending that information via email made me laugh so hard that I ran to the bathroom when I read it.

Now I was sitting in Peru, laughing again. Her treatment of such serious news in the form of an email tells you everything there is to say about my father; nothing surprised any of us anymore. We had all had it with him, but for Shana to throw her hands up was particularly amusing. It was like a priest finally declaring, "Yes, I do want a hit of that joint. Enough is enough."

Later, when Shana and I spoke on the phone, she filled in some details of how she confronted my father about his illegitimate son. This was the scene that played out for me word for word, in a real-time pace, during the ayahuasca trip. It was like watching a play.

"So, Dad, I got a call from Anthony," Shana said.

"Who's that?"

Shana was walking with the pizza that had just been delivered and plopped it on my father's lap as he sat on the beach towel.

"Your son. The son you had before you married Mom.

The woman you told to take a hike when she came to you to tell you she was pregnant? Anthony?"

"Oh, Tony," he said, as if they spoke about him regularly. Then he opened the pizza box and asked, "Why is it full pepperoni, when I asked for half mushroom, half pepperoni?"

"Pepperoni, Dad? I got a call from your son Anthony today. Do you know who that is?"

"Ah, Anthony. What did he say?"

"What did he say?" she screamed at him. "What did *he* say?!"

My sister doesn't have one iota of incredulity in her day-to-day life. She never screams or yells or throws fits. She never loses her temper. She's a nurse, and she's soft and nice and sweet, just like my mother was.

"What do *you* have to say, Dad? What do *you* have to say for yourself?" Shana screamed at him. "You have another son whose mother came to you and told you she was pregnant and you blew her off, and this kid has grown up with a father who raised six other children, without ever acknowledging him? How do you think that made him feel? How could you not care about your own son? What is wrong with you, and how many other Anthonys are out there?"

"What else did he say?" my dad asked, unperturbed, trying to angle two stuck-together pieces of pizza into his piehole.

"Who?"

"Anthony," he clarified, recovering one of the pieces of pizza that had fallen on the beach towel. "What else did Anthony say?"

"No, Dad. My question is: *What do* you *have to say?* What do *you* have to say for yourself?!"

This was one of my favorite moments for Shana. She was finally standing up for something. She was fighting. She had had enough, and she was fierce. She had outrage. I sat there in my hut in Peru, beaming. And then—it hit me.

The realization that I liked my sister the most when she acted the way I would have. *Oh, my God.*

My sister had my outrage; she just used it more sparingly. My way wasn't the only way and it wasn't the right way. There are many ways.

As soon as that clicked in, the images stopped and reshuffled.

The next thoughts in my head were telling me that it was okay to be by myself. That I didn't need so many people around me all the time. That I was enough on my own, and that more time alone would be good for me. That there was too much clatter, too many people always swirling in and around my life—that happiness can come without all that noise, and that I can choose to find that happiness alone.

Ironically, this was happening at the same time I was contemplating going downstairs to tell the crew and Molly what had just happened. I was hearing that I had a choice to stay and see where this would take me or to default to my comfort zone, which has always been and most likely always will be socializing. The voice was my own subconscious, telling me, *It's okay to be alone, it's a choice you can make,* while the other part of me was thinking, *But I really want to go downstairs and hang out with my friends.*

I had made a huge discovery, and for me that was enough.

"I'm good," I said, opening my eyes. Then I got up, wiped the tears off my face, went downstairs, ordered a vodka on the rocks, and told everyone what had happened.

. . .

I loved my experience with ayahuasca. Ayahuasca doesn't make you feel euphoric. It's not like Ecstasy, where you feel sexual and open and you love everyone. It isn't a social drug; it is a solitary experience. I remember every minute of it. I had this overwhelming feeling of love, and a feeling of looking at my life outside of my life. A total shift in perspective. It's a wake-up call, and I can see how it saves people. Ayahuasca isn't a drug I would recommend for everyone. If you have dark thoughts, it could take you down a dark path, but if you don't have a fearful disposition and are fairly open-minded, there's a chance you could get something giant out of it. A metanoia.

. . .

My sister and I didn't get along when we were growing up, but not because she was a bitch. She wasn't. She was just shy, and I was the asshole. I thought she was lame. She thought I was the Devil. I remember sitting in my room, twirling my make-believe mustache, plotting how I was going to stay one step ahead of her. It was definitely more of a feeling than a specific memory. It was more of an overall vibe—I couldn't trust her, and I felt like she was always holding me back.

She tattled on me a lot, and I hated that. I've often thought that maybe we were just born in the wrong order.

I should have been older, and she should have been the youngest. She wouldn't have felt so threatened by me, and I wouldn't have stolen her thunder, or been so spoiled. I would have known what it was like to look after someone else instead of always looking out for myself.

My sister is quiet-funny. She's not like me. Where I roar, she giggles. I always wanted adventure. Shana always wanted safety and security. She has always had this little-girl feel about her, whereas I was forty the day I was born. Rough, loud, and unapologetic. Shana was quiet, shy, and careful. She was a virgin until she met her husband. I lost my hymen in the womb.

My sister just wanted to be my sister, and it was a giant epiphany for me to come to that realization. She needed my love, and I was being selfish. I lacked empathy. Again.

. . .

One thing that stands out so prominently about my childhood: my mother favored Shana, and I knew it was because Shana needed it. I had no jealousy about that. Shana drove me crazy because I thought she was a prude and a tattletale, but I was never jealous of her. It was more along the lines of, *When are you going to stop playing the trumpet, and be cool?* I didn't know then that the trumpet *was* cool.

Because I wasn't jealous of her, it never occurred to me that she might be jealous of me. She had been the baby for five years before I was born; she was living the high life, until I steamrolled right over her, sucked up all the energy, and left her in the dust. I didn't know the feeling of being jealous when I was that young, because there was no one to be jealous of. Shana was always in my rearview mirror. She was never in my way, but I was always in hers.

. . .

My ayahuasca experience came before I started seeing Dan. I wonder what would open up if I did it again, now that I am so much more aware of my blind spots. I know so much more than I did a year ago. I know to wait. I know to listen more than talk. I know silence isn't deadly—it's strong. I know that I lack empathy, and I need to look out for it.

When I came out of the hut, I found our director and Molly standing by the monitor. Molly was crying and holding her arms out to hug me.

"It was all good," I reassured her. "Nothing sad; it was all about Shana. That I need to love her more."

"It was so strange watching you crying, but smiling and laughing the whole time. I thought for sure you were having a mental breakdown, and we were going to have to carry you out of here on a stretcher, but you just seemed so happy," she said, sniffling.

That is Molly in a nutshell. If she loves you, you will know it and feel it every single day you're alive. She is one of nine children, and treats every one of them—as well as both her parents—like they are the eye of the storm. She does this for her boyfriend, she does this for me, she does this for Karen, and she probably does this for a bunch of people I've never even met. She shows up when you need her, and sometimes even when you think you don't—and she stays. She is filled with love. "Stuffed" would be a more apt way to describe it. Stuffed with love.

I didn't tell Shana about my experience with the aya-huasca. What I did was change my behavior toward her. I was easier on her, I confided in her more, and I exercised more patience.

When she saw the documentary, she called me and told me she had noticed a change in my behavior and now she knew why.

"That was so sweet," she told me. "I have totally noticed a difference."

That's my sister. Just loving, and happy to be a part of things. Easygoing. Qualities I had never given any thought to, or admired. No demands for an apology. No hard feel-ings. Well, maybe there are hard feelings, but no feelings are hard enough to erase the deep love and understanding she will always have for me, and that I realized I needed to have for her.

Now I trust her. She trusts me too. It was worth all of that to get here. These are the more vivid memories any-way. The higher notes. I could've watched us as children playing in the water for hours.

When we did finally talk about how she had confronted my father about his son Anthony, she said, "I'm glad you saw what happened with Dad. Can you believe how laissez-faire he was about the whole thing?"

"What an asshole," I told her.

"I almost took the piece of pizza and slapped him across the face," Shana went on.

"Why didn't you?" I asked her. "That would have been great for my ayahuasca highlight reel."

. . .

There are sisters. And then there are sisters. My sisters and I have covered a lot of ground. It shifts. Simone was always a mother figure, and then at some point our roles reversed and I became the older sister. I don't know if Simone sees it that way, but that's the way I see it. She took care of me for so long that somewhere along the way it became time for me to take care of her.

Now when I need someone, it is Shana I go to for comfort.

The last time I was really upset, she somehow had a sixth sense something was wrong and called me first.

"Is everything okay?" she asked. "You haven't posted anything on Instagram for a couple of days."

When I got done telling her what had happened, she asked me if I had told Molly or Karen yet.

"No."

"Have you told Simone?" she asked.

"I don't know that anyone can help me with this," I told her.

"I agree," Shana said. "Let's just keep this between us." My sister was showing up for me, and I was happy to have her.

MOVING
HILLSIDES

"I think I've figured some stuff out," I told Dan, who sat across from me as I peeled the orange he'd handed me, the way a normal adult person would—without juice squirting into my eyes or Dan's, without stabbing the orange with my fingernails, without acting like a gorilla.

After eight months of cultivating self-awareness and some considerable self-reflection, I realized I had arranged my life so that people would always have to know where I was. Whether I was getting on a plane or getting into a car, there were always people picking me up and dropping me off and checking to make sure I was where I was supposed to be. None of my TV shows and stand-up shows and books could happen without me, so all of the people who worked on those things depended on me. Without me, everyone else wouldn't be in the building. I had created a life in which my clothes were chosen for me, my time was scheduled for me, my hair and makeup were done daily. I had regressed into childlike behavior after positioning myself at the center of everyone's universe, so that, finally, everyone had to know where I was, and if anything happened to me, it would all come to an end. I had created a life in which I was finally being pampered—or parented.

I remember the feeling I had when I was walking to the set to do one of the very first episodes of *Chelsea Lately*, and I heard my stage manager on his walkie-talkie say, "She's walking." I loved that there was a coordinated effort to make sure I was where I was supposed to be. I remember being backstage at Radio City Music Hall and hearing the stage manager say, "She's ready to start the show. I'm walking her to stage." I remember one of my attorneys telling me the E! network was thinking about taking out an insurance policy on me, in case I was injured during one of my ski trips—because, well, I did get injured. Instead of feeling like livestock, I felt like I mattered. My parents would never have thought about doing such a thing— insuring me. Years and years of being looked after by teams of people wherever I went meant that I was finally important.

"That's pretty big," Dan told me.

"This is why I've carved out an existence where most people involved in my life are being paid to take care of me. I created a structure that I could inhabit, that would house my need for constant chaos. I could surround myself with chaos, while always remaining in charge of it. Consistency was unfamiliar territory—therefore dangerous—so if things were going well for too long or became predictable, my impulse would be to disrupt—move on and out. Make noise."

Dysfunction was my junction. Function felt off, like water in my ears.

"You were doing all of this unconsciously," Dan said.

"Why do people say 'unconsciously'? Isn't it 'subconsciously'?" I asked him. "'Unconsciously' implies that you're not even awake. Doing something without thinking—isn't that 'subconsciously'? Being awake and not thinking?"

"Yes, actually. I suppose that's true, but people just choose to use 'unconscious' more."

"Why, though?" I asked as I neatly stacked the orange peels on a tissue in my lap.

"I don't know." He shrugged.

"Sorry, I get into word arguments a lot. Mostly with myself. Well, that's not true. I correct people all the time. I also need to stop doing that. Like when people say 'anyways.' The word is 'anyway.' 'Anyways' is not a word. My reaction to 'anyways' is similar to my reaction to room temperature water. I know, however, that this is my overcompensation for never having gone to college, so we don't really need to dissect it."

"Okay, so back to your being looked after . . ."

"Yes, I've infantilized myself."

"And how did that feel, having everyone know where you were?"

"Great, because I was the adult and the baby at the same time. But, eventually, I got sick of that too. Too many people up my ass all the time. It's like I want people to be thinking about me—but not to be in my face about it. Everything with me is black or white. All or nothing."

"Life or death," Dan said. Dan is very calm and talks a lot about being present. He doesn't have a lot of sarcasm, and he is slightly unsure about what to do with mine. He is sixty and somewhat slight, and always comes rushing in to our appointment from outside a little windswept, key ring jingling. Ironically, I'm always there ten minutes early, waiting for him—a nice benefit of never having been picked up on time as a child; I never want anyone waiting for me, because I know what that feels like. *Hang on—is that empathy?*

I asked Dan if he thought I had ADD—or maybe I claimed to have it so that he wouldn't have to waste his time diagnosing me with it. He didn't think I had ADD, but it seemed to him that when I wasn't interested in something, I had trouble pretending I was. This was not news. He told me I could take the actual test for ADD, but that it took eight hours.

"That's never going to happen. Let's just assume I have it."

"I don't think you have it, and I would have a very good sense, after sitting with you all these hours, if you did have ADD. You are a person who is very interested—in what you are interested in."

"I'm interested in being less spoiled."

"Why?"

"Because I can do better."

"Being spoiled is symbolic more than anything," he told

me. "You just explained beautifully that you want people to take care of you, so you're always looking to fill that need, because it's something you didn't have growing up—adult supervision and reliability."

It felt good to start contributing to our dialogue in a concrete way. My favorite pursuit in the world is to sit around and shoot the shit with someone smarter than me. It made me feel like I was playing good tennis.

. . .

At our next session, Dan asked me where I saw myself in five years.

Just when I thought we had been making progress and that he understood who he was dealing with, I had to wonder if he had been listening to anything I said.

"Five *years*? I don't have a five-day plan. I've always assumed I'll be dead in five years, no matter what year it is. Not in a macabre way or anything. I feel like I've had a full life. Like, this has been awesome. Things have been pretty easy, minus the death stuff. I've still managed to have a blast. I have great friends, family," and then I stopped when I realized I was eulogizing myself.

"And you don't want children?"

I gave Dan the same exasperated look I gave him when he asked me about my five-year plan. I felt like this was a good opportunity to bring up patience.

"I'd like to talk about my lack of patience. It's like God skipped me."

"How so?"

"Because that question irritates me, because we've discussed this already, and I feel agitated. That can't be a normal state. Constant agitation."

"Why are you agitated?"

"Because I don't like repetition. We've covered it. The same reason I've never read a book twice. Once I've gotten something, it holds little interest for me."

"Well, you move fast."

"Right. I need to exercise more patience. How do we do that? I'm spoiled and I'm entitled. I'd like to dial that all back."

"Tell me what you mean, exactly."

"If something takes too long, I just move on. I lose interest. I can't deal with electronics or technology or people who work in airports. Basically, anything that takes too long. If there is a line at a magazine store in an airport, I'll just wave twenty dollars up in the air so the airport security cameras catch it and then I'll place it near the register and walk out with whatever item I've taken. I can't deal with the slowness of the transaction. It drives me up a fucking wall."

"Well, that is spoiled," Dan told me.

"Isn't that more entitled?" I asked him. "A black person wouldn't feel comfortable doing that."

"I've never heard of anyone doing that," Dan told me. "By the way, that's empathy." He pointed at me. "Thinking about what it's like to be a black person. You're learning."

"Empathy couched in my entitlement. How convenient."

"You're talking about becoming a systems thinker versus a linear thinker. To be able to look at the macro rather than the micro."

"Yes. I've been like this for a long time, and I don't know if I can blame that on Chet dying. I'd like to, but I'm pretty sure I was throwing temper tantrums as a little girl before he died. I was always a bit of a hot mess."

"It makes sense when you were a little girl, because you were trying to get your parents to pay attention. Even before Chet died, it seemed the two of you already had an understanding about your parents' lack of parenting, so it was in your consciousness."

"Or my unconsciousness."

"Or your subconsciousness." He smiled.

"The question is: Why am I so impatient as an adult?"

"Okay," Dan said, in his wonderfully measured way. "Give me an example of something that happens frequently."

"When I can't turn on the TV in my house—or I can't get the music on—that's something that happens all the time, and then I have to call Brandon or Tanner. Whoever's got the night shift."

This felt less like tennis and more like Ping-Pong, but if Dan wasn't looking at me funny, I wasn't going to be looking at me funny either.

"What does it feel like when you can't work your music?"

"Annoyed."

"What's underneath that?"

"More annoyance."

"But what's the emotion under it?" he persisted.

"I don't know. Anger?"

"What does it feel like?"

"Can't you just tell me?"

"Keep going. Are there any images that elicit the feeling?"

I had no idea what Dan was talking about. "Musical notes?" I asked, searching.

"Is there a feeling?"

"Frustration."

"Because, why?"

"Because my intention was to listen to music, and now I can't."

"Anything else?"

"Stupid?" I asked. "Useless?"

"Helpless?"

"Yes!"

"And what does that feel like?"

"Sad?"

"Sit with that."

"Helpless and sad," I agreed, "but then where does the anger come in?"

"Sad is your internal reaction, which turns to anger because anger sets you in kinetic motion to avoid the sadness of sitting there and not listening to music, and knowing your plans have been thwarted. Your anger is your way to avoid sadness."

"Hold on. Let me write that down." I didn't have a pen.

"You were a helpless little girl who had parents that left you alone too much. When something doesn't go your way, you get angry because you feel that helplessness."

"So, what is my exercise to stop this behavior?"

"Identification. Awareness. Modification. Or, if you like acronyms—IAM." Dan was the one who liked acronyms, so I had no choice but to start liking them too. My life had become filled with acronyms and wheels.

"You identify the internal emotion you are feeling when something upsets you or doesn't go your way. You stop, take a breath, and become aware of it. Then you simply modify your behavior—and/or your reaction. You may find that after you give it some space, you may not want to react at all."

"Yes, I've heard about people doing that."

"Are you ever able to sit back when you've heard a story more than once, or know the person you're speaking to is wrong about something, but you withhold?" Dan asked.

Dan was talking about impulse control. He may as well have been speaking Portuguese.

"Does impulse control go with empathy? Because I don't have that one either."

I came to understand that motion had been cemented in my life at a time when I needed it to survive, and over time it became the only way I knew. It was my oxygen. I didn't know how not to move fast, or how not to state my opinion, or how to just observe something rather than insert myself.

"But all that action doesn't coincide with my sleep schedule," I pointed out. "How is it that I can't stop moving, but I also want to hibernate and withdraw? I can sleep for twenty hours straight, well . . . if I take a Xanax."

"Because you're exhausted."

"Oh, right. Sorry, that was a dumb question." This was a stimulating conversation. Things were clicking into place. "Well, this explains why I can't shut the fuck up."

"Well . . ."

"The other day, I was on my way into the airport when I heard about Trump undoing a ban on some terrible fertilizer that enlarges children's brains—the company who makes it donated one million dollars to his inaugural committee."

"Okay . . ."

"When I walked into the lounge, I headed straight to the little section that plays Fox News, hoping to find someone I could excoriate for continuing to support Trump. I can't go on like this."

"Well, that particular issue isn't an unreasonable thing to have anger about."

"Okay, fine, but I don't want to be filled with such vitriol for Trump supporters. I want to be able to listen, and not always insert myself when there are things I disagree with. Not just with Trump supporters. With everything."

Now that I had identified the genesis of my anger, I could better articulate what I wanted so badly to get out of this therapy experience: I wanted to learn how to be quiet.

My plan after ending my Netflix show was to travel the country and speak to people who had points of view and experiences different from my own. To understand why people continued to support Donald Trump. To do something—besides sitting around on my soapbox and complaining. I was getting so much more out of therapy with Dan than anything else I had ever done in my life. I was being heard, and I didn't even have to yell.

"I'd like to order a scoop of quiet determination," I told Dan. "I've only ever had the loud kind. I want to listen more and talk less. Rectitude without the self-righteousness."

Dan told me to be reasonable with myself. To know that you don't break habits overnight, and that being aware of your bad habits is half the battle. It's downhill after you identify what your bad habits are.

He told me not to be a perfectionist about it. I had to slow down and go through the process of change. Identification. Awareness. Modification.

"Just so you know, I'm not a perfectionist. Whatever the opposite of a perfectionist is—that's what I am. Is there a word for that?"

"Not that I know of," he told me. "So, you're not a perfectionist. You're winging most things."

"Some things come easily to me, but some things are much harder for me than for the average person. Silly things. Like I need very specific instructions to do anything technological."

"Do you quit those things easily?"

"Usually once I get good at something, I lose interest. Sometimes, I lose interest in things before they even happen. I feel like I'm on a Tilt-A-Whirl."

"Once the challenge is gone, you probably feel like you're idling. It's the need for motion. The need for doing."

"Yes, I try hard in the beginning. I won't give up. It took me over a hundred tries to get up on a wakeboard for the first time—in my thirties. Even the two guys driving the boat were exasperated with me after two hours, and tried to convince me to take a break. My body was sore from being pulled in so many different directions during every wipeout. By the time I got up on the wakeboard, I looked back at the big boat, where hours earlier all my friends had been cheering me on, and everyone had gone inside."

We stared at each other for a short while, and then I started to laugh. "Seems to be a recurring theme in my life. Performing for people who aren't even watching."

"Or performing for a lot of people who are watching."

"Performing in general," I said.

The expression on Dan's face I see the most is the one where he looks sad but hopeful for me—like he's rooting for me.

"But you got up," he said.

"Yes, I got up, and now I can water-ski *and* wakeboard topless. You can probably watch it on YouTube."

· · ·

That particular morning, I felt strong. I felt strong because all of the previous sessions where I'd cried and cried had fortified me. For the first time, I felt like someone who was able to pair my strength with my newfound vulnerability. I felt strong because I was able to recognize the behavior that I had adapted as my cover and I knew I could handle unraveling more.

Dan asked me about my relationships with men.

I told him about my two serious relationships, and he commented that it was odd for someone my age who is out and about, successful, and physically presentable (and also penetrable) not to have had more long-term relationships. It was an atypical thing for Dan to say to me, because he wouldn't normally say anything that was in the same hallway as judgment.

"Why is it odd?" I asked him.

"I think people your age have, on average, been in more than two adult relationships."

"Isn't that my need for constant newness? Constant stimulation?"

"Dopamine," he told me.

Relationships without hiccups were too boring, so inevitably they had to end. *Don't get comfortable.* Uncomfortable and not knowing had become my comfort zone. I was always looking for an ultimatum—a way to test someone's commitment, to prove they would disappoint me, and if they didn't do anything wrong, I would find a way to prove they were disappointing before they even had a chance to be.

"Yes, so my inclination has been to have casual relationships around the world with different men—so when I'm in Spain, there's someone, when I ski, there's someone, and then there's someone I can travel with, although I haven't found that person yet. I also know now that my fear of deep intimacy is because of what happened to my brother and my father—both disappearing in different ways. That the feelings I've clung to for so long are most likely self-preservation, believing I am all alone in this world, and all I have to depend on is me."

"Do you feel like you have issues with intimacy?" Dan asked.

"I have a love/hate relationship with intimacy. Intimacy to me always feels like it occupies a narrow space between honesty and being horny. I don't conflate sex with intimacy. Intimacy implies trust, and if trust is broken, then the intimacy was never real to begin with. So, in my experience, there's false intimacy and then there's the other one, which is the best feeling in the universe, and it's not just about being in love with someone you're attracted to—it's the feeling of someone who sees you and loves you right back. The way you don't have to wear a hat for your best friends and family." *Or the person you are paying to help detangle you.*

"Do you want to be in a relationship?" Dan asked.

"Sometimes I think I do—but I don't know for sure. Eventually, everyone ends up annoying me. Everyone ends up talking too much, being too sentimental, overstating their opinions, basically everything that annoys me about myself."

"Have you ever had your heart broken?"

"Yeah, that's annoying too."

"Would you like to talk about that?"

"Not really, because now that we have gone through what my real issues are, all the male relationships in my life seem irrelevant. People I've given multiple chances to probably didn't deserve them, and the people that deserved a second chance didn't get one. I seem to have gotten my signals crossed somewhere along the line. Now I know that it's because I've been in perpetual motion. I've been moving so fast, I can't even see straight."

"You have been a human doing, and we need to get you to be a human being."

"Did you really just say that sentence?" I winced.

"Why, what's wrong with that sentence?" he asked innocently.

"It just sounds like something straight out of a therapist's handbook," I told him.

This felt like a golden opportunity to alert Dan to some non-negotiables I had regarding men.

"Bear with me," I told Dan. "This is going to be a long list. I don't like strong scents, so that kind of prohibits waking up next to someone of the opposite sex, or any sex, really. I'm extremely sensitive to smell. I have a problem with smelling anyone's breath. I'm not the kind of person who can get past that. I get turned off very easily. It could be anything. It could be finding out they have a cat, or seeing their apartment, or they could love room temperature water."

"What else?"

"Feet are tricky. That's why I like to lead with them. When I meet a guy I like, I take out a foot and show him what he'll be dealing with if things go any further. Put your worst foot forward. That's how I like to start a conversation. And then, when they're gracious enough to tolerate me and my feet, God forbid they have a weird foot or a double-decker toe—I can't deal with it."

Dan was squinting at me. "Is there something wrong with your feet?"

"No, but they're feet . . . feet can be tricky in general."

"Okay, let's keep moving," he said with a sigh.

"Also, I have too many questionable habits that no man would be cool with, and by the way, if there was a guy that was cool with them, I'm not sure I'd be interested in him. There are snacks I get in the middle of the night that are not something I could do if anyone was around. If I didn't have cleaning ladies that came every day, I'd probably be in jail. I find crumbs everywhere. In my clothing. My bed. My cleaning ladies leave chocolate next to my bed like I'm at a hotel, and those usually end up somewhere in my sheets. I don't have a flawless enough body to get away with some of the more disgusting things I do . . . or eat . . . in bed. This is all from my mother. She ate in bed all the time, and there's nothing I find more comforting than eating in bed. I stand by it, actually. It's just not ideal for another person to have to witness."

"Anything else?"

Dan looked intrigued . . . or bored. It was hard to tell.

"There are certain accents I simply cannot bear. One of them is my own. I can get icked out so easily. I'm aware this behavior is unreasonable and immature, and I'd like it to stop. I don't want to get turned off so easily, but I just don't know how to get past a bad pair of shoes, or . . . male jewelry."

"Can you give me an example of a specific incident?"

"I could give you a hundred. Pick a city." Dan asked me if I was serious. I was only half serious, but yes, I was serious.

"Let's start with the last guy I hooked up with. Nice guy, nothing wrong with him. I was in Park City—skiing for a few days—and hooked up with a friend of a friend. Anyway, we wake up in the morning, and he tells me he wants to drive me to the airport instead of me taking a car service, because he was heading back to his house in Salt Lake City. I was rushing to pack my things and wasn't thinking clearly—because I said yes, and normally I would not do that."

"Why not?"

"Because I don't want to be in a car with a guy I barely know for that long. It's a forty-five-minute ride to the airport."

"Okay."

"So, we get in the car, and I immediately regret my decision. It was like being on a first date—after we had sex."

"What was so bad about it?"

"Well, we got on the road, and then he lowers the music and says, 'Top ten favorite bands. Name 'em.' "

"And?"

"And that was it. That sentence hurt my vagina. 'Top ten favorite bands'?"

"And then what happened?" Dan asked.

"I told him to turn the music back up so I could find out."

"And that was it?"

"Oh, no. It's never a small story. This ordeal went on for hours. Keep in mind, this was simply a nice guy giving me a ride to the airport that was supposed to be only for forty-five minutes. We got to the airport early, and he insisted on driving me around the area to show me his house, and then he wanted to have breakfast. I felt like I was being held hostage. There was nothing I wanted to do less than have breakfast, and when we got to the restaurant, he ordered an ahi tuna sandwich and a Caesar Bloody Mary. I almost threw up at the table."

"I see."

"This happens all the time. All over the world. It's never just an incident. It always snowballs into something bigger."

"Tell me about the kind of men you do like," Dan said.

"I like older men a lot, and I'll tell you why it's become a problem: because I just turned forty-three, and older men are getting really old, if you catch my drift. So now I have to scale back my margin and lower the difference in age that's most preferable to me, which used to be twenty years. This is what is referred to as 'thinning the herd.' That is why I have the feelings I do for Robert Mueller."

"I'm sorry?" Dan asked.

"I have strong feelings for Robert Mueller. I find him incredibly sexy, and I know why. It's because he has his shit together, and my father never did. I get the psychology behind it, but then I'll hook up with younger guys who are absolute and utter messes—whose lives I turn upside down even more, and who I then lose interest in. These relationships are based solely on their looks and their bodies. It's completely reckless behavior when I think about it.

"My interest in younger men is new, but they have to be grown men. They can't be grow*ing*. I want to be thrown around on a bed (in a loving way) while also being told to shut the fuck up when I'm being obnoxious. I know that's not a popular thing to say in the current climate, but that's what I like. Young guys won't do that. I want to be dominated—by an older man—but in the past couple of years, I've had no choice but to start dipping into younger guys just because that's what the Lord keeps putting before me.

"The real problem with younger men is that I am always the first one to lose interest, and in the past, it has cost me tens of thousands of dollars," I went on. "I've had a few younger guys in my life, and each time I convince myself I'm not going to get sick of them—like a new album you listen to repeatedly. You know if you abuse an album and listen to it too many times, you're going to get sick of it, but part of me always thinks *this* album will be different."

"Why does it cost you money?" Dan asked.

"Because I usually upend their lives in some irreparable way—like I come in and out, and I don't take them seriously, and just want to have fun—and then, when they get serious, I just want to do anything that will make them feel better, so I usually just give them money."

"What?" Dan looked horrified.

"I don't make them sign NDAs or anything. It's not like Trump. It's just more of a parting gift, to lessen the blow. Like a couple guys got fired who worked at resorts where I was a guest—that kind of thing. They weren't supposed to mingle with the guests, so when they get fired, and I'm done with my little fling, I give them money. I know that it's ridiculous behavior, and now I'm just using that money to support strong political candidates, so we don't really have to dissect that either."

"I think we do."

"Yeah, I know you probably think we do, but IAM." I may have winked at Dan when I said this, but I hope I didn't. "Identification. Awareness. Modification. I'm going to modify, so let's keep talking about relationships, because I want to know what's wrong with me. Or what's not wrong with me. Let's ring that bell, shall we?"

"You shouldn't be giving men money just because you are breaking up with them, whether they got fired or not. You're not forcing them to sleep with you, are you?"

"No, Dan. I'm not raping men."

"So, why are you paying them?"

"Because, I'm just not thinking about their circumstances and that they could lose their jobs. So, if that happens, and it has happened, I try to ameliorate the situation—with money."

"Do you understand that that behavior—paying someone to break up with them—is completely unnecessary?"

"Yup."

I needed to switch gears. I told Dan that I also go for very long periods of time without any male interest or sex, and I'd prefer to be having more sex.

"You don't get hit on by men?"

"No. Not typically. Not in America. I think I'm just one big boner killer. Older men like me, because they've seen it all and they probably find it refreshing, but men my own age are definitely not interested."

"Why?"

"Probably because I'm loud. It's obnoxious. People are scared of me."

"You say that often."

"I hear it often."

"People tell you they're scared of you?"

"Dan, I'm loud and brash. Certain people find that off-putting. Most straight men find that off-putting. This isn't hard for me to understand. Why is it hard for you to understand?"

"It sounds like you've worked your entire life to make sure that you wouldn't get hurt again."

"But, I have gotten hurt. I've had my heart broken."

"And what did that feel like?"

"It was awful. I was completely out of control—like a madwoman. I get distracted with love, and I've let it take over before. I've done unreasonable things, like checking a guy's phone, or acting out of fear and jealousy—all the qualities I'm not interested in having ascribed to me. It's just so much safer to be single. I just get more done when I'm single. So, yeah, let's talk about that."

"That's your doing, not your being." I pretended I didn't hear that.

"So, is that Chet too?" I asked Dan. "He's certainly getting a lot of airtime for a dead guy."

"I don't think you'll allow it. I don't think your *sub*conscious thinks it can take another letdown. You are most likely actively making sure that you are preserving the only reliable thing in your life."

"Which is?"

"You."

"Yikes," I said.

"Do you think you're capable of being in a loving, caring relationship with a man, knowing that if something terrible happens, and he dies, that you will be okay?"

"No. No. No. No one can die." Dan stared at me. My body reacted as if I had been Tasered. The tears filled my eyes and spilled down my cheeks. Once that sentence left my mouth, I was able to hear myself. Not what I said, but the tone with which I said it and the age of that voice. The nine-year-old.

"I can die, but no one else can die. It's enough already with death," I said, snapping back to my present-day self.

"Did you feel what happened to your body when I suggested that someone could die?" Dan asked, with his bottom lip curled inward.

"Yeah. I'd rather be alone. I can't take another death."

"I want you to think about what you just said."

No matter how many times our conversations would lead us away from Chet, we'd always end up back there.

Dan was making sure we paused every time Chet came up—he wanted to make sure I didn't minimize my feelings, and he was constantly relitigating my pain back to me—each time further convincing me of the notion that I had a right to be in pain. Not to feel like my pain wasn't valid because I wasn't raped or assaulted or molested or beaten or worse. Just because I grew up with all the things I needed and never had any real perceivable struggle, that didn't preclude me from having the right to unearth my pain. To not power through it and assume it was in my past simply because I'd identified it. He wanted me to live those moments slowly and repeatedly, to make sure the pain didn't get stuck again—to wring it out.

That is not my comfort zone. Hashing, then rehashing, something. I don't like repetition. I like newness. I had to remind myself constantly that this was a reasonable course of action. I was learning from Dan not to object to something without hearing it out or giving it a whirl. I was giving sitting in pain a whirl—and it felt yucky.

Dan explained that in very traumatic times, you freeze.

"You do the only thing you can do to survive the pain, which is to shut off and retreat to your own world, because if you were to absorb the pain from all the people around you or acknowledge your own pain, you wouldn't be able to cope. So, you coped, just like everyone else in your family coped—each in different ways. Your coping mechanism was motion. Do something—anything other than sitting around with your feelings."

"But if everything has been a deflection thus far, and I've been pretending to be someone for this long, at some point didn't I eventually just become that person I've been pretending to be?"

"No," he said firmly.

"People are generally consistent at being themselves," I reminded Dan.

"Not when you're working so hard to change that consistency."

"Okay, well, then I'm going to take a step for you, because you've been working so hard on me. I'm going to say something I never thought would come out of my mouth. I think I'd like to be in an adult relationship." And then I wrinkled my nose as if one of us had just farted.

"You don't have to commit to being in a relationship. You don't have to want to be in a relationship. I'm asking you what you want. Any answer is fine."

"Quite honestly, I've never given it much thought. I'm more worried that liking being alone makes me selfish—selfishness is around the corner from narcissism, and anything is better than being a straight-up narcissist."

"You're not a narcissist," he told me.

"Are you sure?"

"Yes. I'm sure. I deal with narcissists all the time. You are consumed with grief that you have been trying to hide for years. Narcissists are defensive, and you haven't been defensive about identifying your shortcomings. Narcissists have trouble being self-critical."

"Oh, thank God." I exhaled. "I feel about narcissism the same way I feel about HIV. I've always suspected I might have it but was too worried to take the test and have it come back positive."

We sat in silence and let this all sink in.

"I'm a storm chaser," I declared to Dan.

"Well . . . you're the storm," he corrected me.

"Yikes. That's a double whoopsie."

Dan nodded, and we stared.

"More like a hurricane," I added.

"Spinning and spinning, and never landing anywhere," he said.

This was another metanoia.

To know I'm going through something and not try to keep circling around it hoping to avoid going through it. Sitting, and experiencing, and feeling, and not running. To understand that things take time, and to be okay sitting with my pain. To understand the only way through something is through it. Not to rush through life hopscotching over or around it. No one is fully cooked. No person is complete.

"You had some unfinished business," Dan told me. "You are healing now. You are learning how to grow and become a fuller person. This is good."

. . .

A few weeks later Dan returned from a trip to Jackson Hole and told me that he had spoken to one of the park rangers who remembered my brother's death. My jaw clenched, my eyes flooded. I was learning to recognize what happened to me physically when faced with this subject. I became aware of the fight my body would put up to prepare to block the pain.

"What did he say?" I asked Dan, referring to the park ranger.

"That it happens all the time."

So my brother was just a number. A statistic. He was one of many, not anything special. Lots of other people died there too.

"Then why would he even remember it, if it was so common?" I asked Dan, whose intention I know was to make me feel better. "Now he's just a number?"

"It's funny how you see that. I was trying to give you comfort—to know that you aren't the only person that this happened to. That your horrible experience has happened to many other people, and now you're upset that you aren't alone in your pain."

Bingo.

I had forgotten to modify. Identification. Awareness. Modification. Baby steps.

It crossed my mind to pay Dan double for that session, but I remembered this was also behavior that needed to be dropped off at the curb.

NEW
LOVE

I know that in five years it will be politically incorrect to body-shame fat dogs—so I'm going to do it now.

With Tammy gone and Chunk getting older, the writing was on the wall—it was time to get another dog. I went to a rescue two hours north of Los Angeles that specialized in Chow mixes, in search of a new addition to my family. When the older lesbian who owned the place told me about a brother and sister Chow duo that came with the names Bert and Bernice, my eyes started to do cartwheels.

"I don't even need to see them," I told her. "I'll take them both."

The first time I saw them rounding the corner, I almost climaxed right there on the dirt. Bert looked like a minia-ture lion and Bernice was his sidecar—a more petite, more portable version of her big, fat brother. Bert is short for Bertrand, by the way, so I had to take a minute to look up at the sun and marinate in that merriment. Bert had all the trimmings of what I look for in a pet: long hair, weight-management issues, and laziness behind the eyes. Bernice was lacking in all three areas and actually maintained very strong eye contact—something I took as a sign of either intelligence or an addiction to Adderall.

The woman who ran the rescue explained that they would need at least two days to give the dogs all their shots and grooming, and that someone from her organization would have to do a home inspection before they gave me the go-ahead. I respected that, but had no idea what it meant. I would have agreed to let her comb through my taxes with a forensic accountant, if it meant having a brother-sister combo platter named Bert and Bernice. I mean, seriously. Does it get any more real than that?

I left Tanner in charge of answering the woman's questions regarding the adoption, and drove back to Los Angeles, looking forward to the challenge of knowing I was ready for some real doggy parenting this time around. Chunk wouldn't be thrilled with the discovery that I had two more dogs coming home, but I would just explain to him that we were trying to keep families together. Chunk was on whatever mission I was on, whether he knew it or not.

Bert and Bernice arrived on a Friday afternoon, freshly groomed and ready to rumble. If Bert is shaped like a giant turkey—which he is—Bernice is the drumstick. Bernice is superior to Bert in terms of traditional good looks, but traditional good looks aren't what I'm after.

Being that it was my year of self-sufficiency, I gave Brandon and Tanner the weekend off. By Sunday morning, I called Tanner and Brandon and told them to get their asses over to the house. The dogs were insane. I couldn't get them to do anything. They'd run up and down the stairs and act like they wanted to play, but when I got near them, they'd psych me out and outmaneuver me. They were both impossible to wrangle. If I managed to grab Bert and tried to put a leash on him, he'd flinch or snap as soon as I touched his neck. Tying a leash around a dog's midsection also doesn't work, and if you don't believe me, try it. They were skittish and confused, and where there wasn't drool on the floor, there was piss. My house smelled like a chamber pot and looked like the grounds of the Burning Man festival, three days after it ended.

Once Brandon and Tanner arrived, it was revealed upon further family discussion that not only were these dogs not potty-trained, they hadn't lived indoors ever. Somewhere along the way, Tanner had forgotten to disclose this little tidbit of information when he was doing their background check. Brandon almost hit Tanner that day.

"So, they're wildlings?" I asked Tanner.

When I suggested returning the dogs, Brandon lost his temper with me. Losing his temper may be an exaggeration, but he definitely jerked his head in a way I hadn't seen before, deftly completing what very well looked like a 360-degree circle.

"I don't think that's a good idea, Chelsea," Brandon said, continuing his bobblehead motion. "You've had them for two days. The woman knows who you are, and it wouldn't look very good to all the people who think you are this big animal lover. Plus, you can't just quit things every time they get too hard."

I had been through sagas like this before. I had procured dogs that didn't work out that had to be rerouted to friends or relatives. The idea that all of a sudden I could handle two new feral dogs was preposterous.

This was supposed to be my year of self-sufficiency—the year I was going to take back my life from my assistants—and here I was, lacking the fundamental skills to clean dog shit off a carpet, and instead sitting on the floor, crying like Brett Kavanaugh during a Senate hearing.

"Why is it so important for you to learn how to clean up dog shit?" Brandon asked. "You have people you pay to do that. Stop torturing yourself with menial tasks."

"Because!" I wailed. "I'm missing out on culture."

. . .

Brandon spent the day calling around and found a dog trainer who offered an eight-week course, and—very fortuitously—he had two available spots. Brandon offered to inquire about a third spot, and to see if they took adult women. Behavioral training for eight weeks actually sounded enticing—like a finishing school, for forty-year-olds. I needed someone to reteach me how to accomplish simple tasks and combat the domestic amnesia that I couldn't seem to shake. For example, I would love to know where the toaster is hidden in my kitchen, but after living in the house for seven years, it's become one of those questions that is just too embarrassing to ask my housekeeper.

While Bert and Bernice were away at get-better camp, Brandon, Tanner, and I would get videos and updates on their progress, with notes like *Bert passed his first week with flying colors* or *Bernice is now ringing a bell to go outside to potty.* The reports always made it sound like the dogs were right on track, until it was time for them to graduate. That was when we got the call that they had completed their eight-week course, but had failed miserably. The trainer said she couldn't, in good faith, let them come back to me without properly "graduating," and that they would need another eight-week course. By the third time they needed to repeat the eight-week course, I asked Brandon if the trainer was planning on keeping the dogs permanently, and if this was the plan all along—hoping I'd forget.

"No," he reassured me. "She just doesn't want them to come home until they both graduate magna cum laude. She says they have some behavioral issues and that they are getting better, but they're not ready."

"These dogs better be able to roller-skate when they get back. I mean, seriously, Brandon."

"And mix drinks," he added.

That's how I felt about myself. *Getting better, but not quite ready.*

. . .

I didn't mind the dogs' absence so much the first eight weeks, or the second eight weeks, because Chunk and I were on our own for the first time in three years and we were enjoying some serious post-Tammy bonding during that stretch—plus, I was secretly dreading Bert and Bernice's return. But when Chunk passed away over Christmas while I was at Whistler, I texted Brandon and told him that I couldn't return to a house without dogs in it.

Upon the dogs' re-entry, I had some obvious decisions to make. First, I was going to have to shave Bert's body and get down to business. I needed to see precisely what kind of physique I was dealing with under all his matted hair. Once shorn, what was unveiled was the exact body type I was hoping for: tons of different folds, flaps, and pockets of extra meat. His body was a wonderland. This was a dog you could use to hide jewelry in, if the situation arose. Cuddling with Bert was what I imagined kneading dough to be like—hypnotic.

Cuddling with Bernice was a bit more sinister. First, you had to catch her. Once caught, Bernice is easily transportable, so I'd bring her over to my bed or a sofa, where she would submit to a two-minute rubdown. But the moment I stopped petting her, she'd pop up—as if suddenly coming to—and like a squirrel spinning through the air, she'd scurry away. She is much more nimble than Bert and can quickly climb up any hillside or jump off a bed in a way that Bert will never experience. Bert can't jump off a bed; either he'd go straight through the floor or the impact alone would kill him.

Bert is more Scooby-Doo, and Bernice is more honey badger. Bernice doesn't give a shit about anyone. Not me, not my cleaning lady Big Mama, not even the landscaper. She does her own thing; she is an independent thinker. The best time to make inroads is when Bernice is sleeping on her side. If you go in and start to rub her belly, she will kick her leg up and roll onto her back to assist you in petting her. My bonding with Bernice takes place during car rides, listening to political podcasts, and on trips to my office. When Bert isn't around, Bernice is a star. When Bert is around, she's like any other marginalized woman.

Bert is everything I've ever wanted in a dog, except for having the signature Chow personality—which means that one minute he will be sweet and loving, and the next he'll rebuff my advances with a snap or a flinch. His nighttime personality when we are in bed together is all love and affection—it's like sleeping with a giant, lifelike teddy bear—but come morning, when we go downstairs, he becomes Daytime Bert, who shuns me and behaves as if we didn't just spend the entire night in each other's arms. I've had myriad one-night stands—which have also been documented—but never anything quite as degrading. The rejection is fierce.

The first few days the dogs were home, Bert was picking up what I was throwing down, but then things started to shift. In the span of one week, he turned on Brandon, then Tanner, and then me. The only one he chose to have a relationship with was Big Mama.

He'd follow Mama around from room to room every day. If any of us even walked by him, he'd shudder as if we had all taken turns beating him the night before. I couldn't get anywhere near Bert unless I had fifteen minutes to kill, because it was a multipronged process to gain access. First, he would hear me coming and attempt to run away. I use the word "run" for lack of a better term to describe Bert in motion. Bert's movements are more labored, and unexpected—like an elephant starting to run and then giving up. Once he capitulated he'd sit down—with his back to me—and I'd have to make my way very gingerly to the front of his body, using a very soft voice, and then wait patiently for an opening. If he made his version of eye contact—essentially side-eye, head down—I would carefully move my hand underneath his chin and rub his chest for a beat, then I'd work my way around his neck to get to his ears and head. Once I got to his ears, he'd finally give in, and then he would allow me to do almost anything to his body. But if there was no gentle prelude and he saw my hand approach his head to pet him, he'd haul ass in the other direction in search of Mama.

"Jew have to go slow," Mama would tell me over and over again when Bert ran into her arms with his tail wagging and his tongue out. The minute Bert heard Mama arrive at my house each morning, he'd run out my bedroom door, down the steps, and into Mama's arms, where they would literally rub noses for five to ten minutes. It was torture watching the two of them together right under my own roof, and Mama never missed an opportunity to throw it in my face.

"Look," she'd say, smiling, as she walked away from the kitchen and into the living room, swinging her hips with Bert two steps behind, swinging his. "Papa go everywhere Mama go."

. . .

"I can't believe you have to tie your dogs to your bed. That is so pathetic," my friend Allison said one Sunday night over family dinner at her parents' house. She was referring to an Instagram story I had posted the night before of Bert and Bernice in my bed—with their leashes on.

"I don't tie my dogs to my bed," I told the rest of the Azoffs sitting around the dining room table. "Sometimes, with his mood swings, Bert doesn't know what he wants, so I'll coax him up the doggy steps into my bed."

"Coax how?" Allison asked, leading me like a witness.

"With a handgun," I declared, flatly, to everyone at the dinner table. "I bring my dogs to bed at gunpoint."

"You may as well. She uses a leash to get them into her bed," she broadcasted, laughing.

"Repetition, asshole," I told Allison, trying to maintain some dignity. "That's what they teach you in every parenting class."

"You're going to be teaching a parenting class if you don't go back to fucking work soon," Irving said, homemade fried rice flying out of his mouth. The rice was made by their trusty chef, Craig. Craig is not Chinese.

Irving is my manager, but really he is a big-deal music manager who has no interest in anything I do—unless the payment exceeds one million dollars. Allison is Irving's daughter, and although we are not related by blood, we are sissies and we love each other big-time.

No one in the Azoff family really approved of my foray into politics after the election. They thought I was too strident and too amped up about Donald Trump. They thought I was being histrionic. Irving liked to remind me, and anyone else who would listen, that I wasn't making any money zigzagging across the country, speaking at colleges and campaigning for candidates.

"I'm sorry I care about the country I live in," I said, mistaking my chopsticks for my vape pen, and trying to take a hit off one.

"She needs to go back to stand-up," Irving's wife, Shelli, chimed in between bites of spareribs, not looking up.

"Well, I'd rather be hysterical and wrong than be right and wake up to Hitler standing at my door," I declared.

"Oh, Sissy," Allison said as she passed her vape across the table. "Take another hit of this."

. . .

If Chunk read *The New York Times* every morning, and Tammy read the *New York Post*, Bert and Bernice are reading *The Sun*.

I like dogs that can make the distinction between television and reality. Dogs that are excited by other dogs in dog-food commercials are, in my opinion, slow on the uptake. Chunk would never lose his cool and bark at the television. Chunk was barely interested in reality; he certainly didn't have time for fantasy.

Bert is constantly confused by the same things he has done moments before. His memory is so short-term that when I'm gone for a few hours, I have to reintroduce myself every time I come home. The dirty looks he throws my way when I try to gain re-entry into his world are so full of disdain that sometimes I don't even have the stomach for it.

At one point, things got so bad that I considered moving out and getting a small apartment so that Bert could have more time to adjust to his new surroundings without me there.

Bernice is a little more coquettish. When Bernice comes up the stairs to my bedroom, she is quick and agile, and it's almost like she's taunting Bert—showing him what it's like to be quick on your feet. She will come upstairs, but when I reach out my hand to pet her, she'll run away maniacally, as if I'm holding an ax.

When Bert comes up the stairs of his own accord—*which he eventually does even if I don't guide him*—it is slow and deliberate, like a sloth, taking one giant step every thirty seconds. It can take weeks. This happens when the house is dark and he has given up any hope of Mama returning home for the night. I am his second choice, and after months of getting used to this, I take whatever I can get.

It can take a laborious forty-eight hours to get Bert out of his funk after Mama leaves on a Friday. It's what I imagine it must be like to lay bricks. He won't look at me—as if he blames me for her leaving—and if I get underneath the dining room table with him, where he hides, he will turn his head away from me and eventually reconfigure his body so his ass is in my face. He is a moody, moody fuck.

When I realized one day that I could trick Bert into coming out from under the dining room table by turning off the lights and speaking in Mama's accent, I started speaking in a Mexican accent for entire weekends.

Mama was the one who fed them and took them outside every day and went over their training exercises and played ball with them. I was sometimes home just two days a week, so in their eyes, she was their real mother and I was just some slutty au pair who came by every couple of weeks to babysit.

"*Ber-r-r-t, Ber-r-r-t,*" I said, in my best impersonation of

Mama, demonstrating for Allison the challenges I faced as a single parent.

"He resents me for being away all the time," I told her.

"Or he just doesn't remember you."

"Well, then he's pretty dumb."

"Don't say that," Allison said.

"Oh, please. He's a dog; he can't understand me."

"You don't know that."

"I do know it, because of that expression on his face," I said. "He's dumb. Talk about old injuries. Every day is like Groundhog Day. It's like he's permanently concussed."

"Well, I'm just telling you, words have meaning," Allison said.

"Well, then in five minutes, I'll tell him he's smart. He won't even remember this conversation."

Those weren't the only challenges the new dogs posed. It was impossible to get any lingerie on Bert's body. Weeks of making inroads, of sleeping in bed with him, of taking him on walks and in car rides—all of it would fly out the window the minute I tried to pick up one of his paws and slip it through the shoulder strap of something silky. Bernice wasn't obsessed with Mama, so I set my sights on her, which ultimately resulted in her playing dead anytime she saw me coming. Bert doesn't play dead, because Bert is mentally dead.

I even made a play for Mama's seven-year-old son, Guillermo, who comes with Mama to my house on school holidays and when he's sick. I started luring him to my bedroom with videogames and candy, just to demonstrate that I could beat her at her own game. This became an issue when Guillermo started following me throughout the house, wanting to play games all day long. I ended up giving him a hundred dollars to just play the videogames without me.

. . .

Three months into having the dogs, Tanner took Bert to the vet and reported that Bert had gained twelve pounds, weighing in at a whopping seventy-two pounds.

We were given strict instructions when we got the dogs back from their six-month training program that no treats were allowed, because Bert had lost twenty pounds while at training camp and needed to keep the weight off.

"Bert's butt *has* gotten huge," Brandon confirmed. "Someone asked me the other day if he had implants."

That's when I connected the dots: Mama was sneaking Bert food in order to ingratiate herself. For the first time in my adult life, I was the one who had stuck to the rules, and Mama was working undercover. When I confronted her in Spanish, she told me she couldn't understand what I was saying. When I confronted her in English, she lashed out.

"Me? Oh, no, Little Mama," she told me. "I don't give him treats. I stick to the schedule. Do *jew?*" she asked, pointing her finger at me, her other hand on her hip.

"No!" I replied. "Not ever."

"*La verdad?*" she challenged me. "What about all the cookies and chocolate jew eat in bed all the time, Little Mama?" Then she turned on her heel and walked out of the kitchen, with Bert following close behind. The two of their asses walking away from me looked like two giant locomotives leaving the station on twin tracks.

"Little Mama" is what Big Mama calls me when she's correcting my Spanish or telling me how Bert prefers to be petted. In these moments she is talking down to me, but because of all the things that Mexicans have had to suffer since Trump got elected, I feel it's my duty to take one for the team.

Bert had been looking more voluptuous, but by then his fur had started growing back, so it was hard to tell what was fluff and what was reality.

"So, he'll need to go on a diet?" I asked Tanner, disappointed.

Tanner told me they gave Bert a thyroid test and it came up negative, but that the vet also noted that thyroid tests often deliver false negatives.

Honestly. What is one supposed to do with that non-information? Isn't medicine science? Isn't science pretty solid, until we find out that the most recent studies have debunked whatever theory we have been living with as fact for the past forty years? For fuck's sake, when am I ever going to get a straight answer from a vet?

"They also said that Bert is most likely eight years old, but that Bernice seems younger."

"I thought they were from the same litter!" I exclaimed, throwing my hands in the air.

"They are," Tanner confirmed. "I think we need to find a new vet. Again."

"Well, get a DNA test anyway."

Tanner thought I meant that *he* should get a DNA test, but that didn't come to light until weeks later, when he told me he was 81 percent Dutch, and we still didn't know if the dogs were brother and sister—or, for that matter, if they were even Chow Chows.

"They are brother and sister," Mama chimed in that day. "As a mama, I know such things. Bert is just too fat right now. The weight adds age."

"Well, I wonder how that fucking happened?"

"*Amigas*, come on," Brandon interjected. "We're all on the same team here."

"*Estamos nosotros?*" I asked Mama, cocking my head to one side.

"For jears, I watch all jour doggies in this house give jew all the love and attention anyone could want. They love their mama. Chunk never loved me the way he love jew. No matter how much we play, he never love me like he love jew. Tammy, okay, but she was not *my* baby. Bert is my baby. He love me, and I love Bert." Then, in perfect English, she said, "Doggies are not a zero-sum game."

"Sounds like someone just got served," Brandon said, as he made an overhead tennis-serve motion with the wrong hand.

The bottom line was this: If Bert was too fat to get up the stairs and get in my bed to cuddle with me, then what was the point of having dogs to begin with? If Bert was in fact five, or eight, or any of the other ages suggested to me, then we didn't have that long before the stairs would become his nemesis. When Chunk got old, I could carry him up the stairs, but carrying Bert was not physically possible for me. So either Bert had to lose some weight or I needed to move into a ranch house. I put Bert on a diet, and I put my house on the market. Whichever happened first, happened first.

What happened first was that I came home from being

away for five days and found Bert and Mama strutting around the house both wearing ankle weights—two for her and four for Bert. Bert and Mama had started their very own weight-loss challenge, and guess who didn't get the group text? This felt like a blow on two fronts. I loved Mama's big, fat curves, and when she lost weight there was less to squeeze, but I knew on an intellectual level that those feelings were irrelevant. We were now living in a time and place where fondling my cleaning lady was no longer acceptable—no matter how welcome those advances appeared to be. This became a story of not only a weight-loss challenge but a loss of sensory pleasures.

It also became an exercise in patience. I have had an infinite amount of love for all my dogs, but these two were the first ones whose love I had to work for. They operated in absolutes—black and white, no gray, you're in or you're out. I was finally getting a taste of my own medicine.

After a full year, things improved for the most part, but I still don't have the upper hand. Now, when I'm out of town, Mama will send me daily updates about the dogs, because she knows that for the first time in my life I suffer from guilt at not being home a lot, and when I am, she sees me spend hours on the floor with Bert and Bernice, begging them to cuddle with me. She knows how much I love Bert's big, fat ass—probably because it's the view I'm most familiar with—so she is always sure to send me one picture from the front and one from the back.

I send her pictures of Bert sitting at her office door after she has left for the afternoon, awaiting her return. She claims she no longer gives Bert treats, and I claim I no longer give Bert treats, but we both know the other is lying.

If I'm gone for a few days in a row, sometimes Mama will send me a full body shot of herself in lingerie, just to tide me over.

. . .

If someone logged the amount of time I spend petting Bert and Bernice, I'd probably be arrested. I'm not going to pretend I don't like Bert's body more than Bernice's—because I have a type—but I *love* them both the same. It's hard for me not to molest my dogs. I know that if I squeeze them as tight as I want to, I'll cut off their circulation. If I had gotten Bert before I met Dan, and not learned about impulse control, Bert would probably be dead.

I didn't know the snugglefest I was missing out on, because Chunk and Tammy were both affectionate, but they weren't hedonists. Neither was interested in drawn-out body rubs and would always at some point politely let me know they were done being petted by me.

Bert is the type of dog that could wake up to a beer every morning and then walk directly into a massage parlor for twenty-four hours straight. If I stop petting Bert, he will tap me on the shoulder with one of his paws and start whining. If Bernice comes up onto the bed, Bert will reposition his body to face away from her, because he is very jealous and wants attention only for himself. Every morning when Bert wakes up, the fur beneath his eyes is soaked. This dog is so lazy that he is literally drooling out of his eyes while he sleeps. Mama will wipe the tears off his face, on average, three times a day. Bert is the epitome of male privilege at its core. Pure, unadulterated privilege. He is the neediest dog I've ever had, and when I hold his body like a giant baby lion in my arms, it feels almost as if he were genetically engineered for me. "Are you my little fat fucker?" I'll whisper to Bert once I've got him in a supine position, or, "I love the way your weight is distributed." I say these things in Spanish because no one in my house speaks English anymore.

It took me a while to get past the fact that when Bernice cleans herself, it sounds like a car wash. Or that Bert sounds like a warthog when you turn him on his back, find the fat flaps underneath his two front armpits, and fondle his soft fur—after rearranging his body in whatever position gives me the most pleasure. I have woken up some mornings with him still in my arms from the night before. Something I never knew was possible . . . until Bert.

It's pretty remarkable to lose two dogs you love so much, only to find out that you can love two new dogs in a completely different way. It made me wonder—how many more kinds of love was I missing out on?

These two fuckers made me step up my parenting. Chunk and Tammy were along for the ride, whereas I'm the one along for Bert and Bernice's ride. I still travel all the time, but when I'm home, I deal with the dogs. I take them for walks and I pick up their dog shit. I'm the one who goes home now for their mealtimes, and I'm the one who takes them to the park. The last part of that sentence is not true. It feels awesome to parent and to know that my parenting matters. That these dogs do not love me unconditionally, and they will not spoil me with love. That we are on a day-to-day basis, and I have to work hard every day to prove to them that I am worthy. That I will be consistent and that my love is not contingent on them loving me the same way I love them. Have I turned into a stalker? Yes. Yes, I have.

. . .

I once fell out of a seaplane and into the Hudson River. I was flying out of Manhattan to visit a friend upstate. After the plane landed, there was a little rowboat waiting to ferry us back to the dock. I slipped stepping into the boat and landed in the Hudson River in my boots, jeans, sweater, and wool peacoat. It was Thanksgiving weekend and we were less than ten feet from shore. You know those babies being taught how to swim in YouTube videos where they are bundled up in sweaters and boots? That's what I looked like. It was freezing and it was funny. Chunk bypassed the little rowboat too and jumped right into the water after me.

Bert and Bernice are never going to rescue me. Even if Bert tried, he'd drown. Bernice would probably just look the other way.

MARIJUANA KEEPS FAMILIES TOGETHER

Some people are not built for drugs and alcohol. I believe that I am. I believe I am built for the apocalypse.

I reconnected with marijuana in my late thirties. As I've previously shared, I'm open to most drugs as long as they don't leave you with a hole in your arm, or staring through a keyhole of an apartment door, looking out for drones. At this stage of my life, I find it prudent to avoid apartments altogether.

I loved pot when I first discovered it in high school—or pretended I did, because I thought it made me look cool—but after a few years of recreational abuse, it just ended up leaving me paranoid and self-conscious, and in one instance, getting up to leave the theater when a movie ended, only to realize I was on an airplane.

Then, one year, my family and I were on our annual

Christmas ski trip to Whistler, Canada, and our chef made special "adult" cookies. Every night, my brothers and sisters would line up in the kitchen on our way to dinner, and I would dole out half of a cookie to each of them—and if any of my nieces and nephews stole any without me seeing, it was none of my business. Our family thrived that year. Our family doesn't really fight, because we're all so exhausted from our childhoods, but it definitely marked the beginning of a new era for the Handlers.

. . .

The legalization of marijuana in California raised standards at dispensaries. The educative component that was lacking for so many years was now available on all store-bought weed. The labeling of strains, along with the labeling of THC vs. CBD ratios, was all right there in black and white. With the advent of medicinal-grade, controlled micro-dosing, there aren't a lot of people I wouldn't recommend it to. I've turned straight-arrow people into people I can actually spend time with. I've gotten friends who have never done any drugs, friends who have had terrible experiences with edibles, my Mormon sister, people's parents, Muslims, and one nun to imbibe. About ninety percent of the people I've introduced to marijuana are now frequent users. I take a lot of pride in being an enabler or, a term I'd like to coin, a "pharmacological intuitive"—one who instinctually knows the exact right dosage for each consumer.

After Trump was elected I came the closest I'd ever been to depressed. My anger rose to the surface, rather than simmering just beneath it. I had something identifiable to be angry about. So, instead of masking it, I treated it.

That's when the news started to get fun. Kellyanne Conway, stoned, is a good time. It's up there with Eddie Murphy's *Raw*. Same for Sarah Suckabee Sanders. One day, Sarah Suckabee Sanders came out for her press briefing with emerald-green eye shadow shrouding one eye, and zero eye shadow on the other eye. I'd find myself laughing when Chris Matthews would interrupt his guests while spitting all over them, and I started to see the news for what it was: a twenty-four-hour spin cycle filled with conjecture and speculation about whatever idiotic or racist comment Trump had tweeted that day. I realized that I had allowed this administration to rob me of one year of my life, and I wasn't going to give them another. I needed a channel change.

The thing that non–cannabis users fail to recognize is the way cannabis bends your frame of mind. It allows access to a recessed part of your brain that I, particularly, was deeply needing to engage. How to be less reactive, how to sand down the edges—these were things I had been working on with Dan. As a result, things became slightly more poetic. Less final, less "end of an empire." My sleep got better, my moods got better, even my dreams got better. I stopped watching the news on a loop, and I even started waking up laughing. Pot, politics, and Dan summed up 2018 for me. The year I had to fall apart in order to come back together.

• • •

I was sitting in Dan's office one Monday morning, telling him how passionate I had become about this new marijuana renaissance.

"My opinions have always felt fully formed," I told Dan.

"With pot, it feels like they are finally unfurling. Every canvas is blank. Everyone is so much less annoying and everything is a little more tolerable when I'm a little bit stoned," I explained. "I also don't feel compelled to talk as much, and with my voice, that's a bonus."

"In what way is everyone so *annoying*?" It was always funny to hear Dan use "annoying" in a sentence. "Annoying" seems like a word that expires after adolescence, like "conceited." I liked that I was finally rubbing off on Dan.

"The thing I'm realizing, Dan," I said, leaning on one elbow, but missing the arm of the chair and falling into my own lap, "is that *I'm* the one who's annoying. It's like, I'm just now finding out, this whole time, I've been the annoying one."

Dan stared straight at me, and it was hard to discern his take on my new hobby.

"I used to think that something was wrong with everyone, and now that I know I'm the one with the problem, everyone seems a lot more interesting," I explained.

"I don't think you should judge yourself so harshly," Dan said. This was a phrase Dan repeated to me frequently, and one I've never quite gotten on board with.

"I do," I told him. "I feel like that's what's been missing this whole time. Circling around other people in order to avoid myself. I deserve to be on the receiving end of my own judgment. It's my comeuppance.

"It's like this little porthole into a whole new world has opened up," I continued. "When I'm stoned, I can find joy in shaving my legs."

This was when I realized I *was* stoned. I had popped a chocolate-covered Kiva blueberry on my way out the door that morning. I don't usually take them in the morning, but I had therapy and thought—*Why not?* That's my favorite thing about edibles: forgetting you've taken some, then feeling a little psychological twinkle, and suddenly things get just a wee bit more dynamic. Weed lit up my curiosity in things I hadn't had interest in for years. That's what I was missing—getting lost in life a little more.

Dan told me that if I could access that state of mind when I was high, it was already part of my psyche—which meant that I could access it without anything at all, or through meditation.

"I'm not there yet," I said. I had been trying for months to meditate, and it was going nowhere, fast. I could only do forced meditation when I was with Dan. He made me short recordings and long recordings, and I'd try it for a few days at home, and then forget, or remember—and then forget.

"Not only is it easier for me to be around people, it's definitely easier for people to be around me. I am able to have conversations with people I never had the patience to listen to before. I'm so much less judgmental. Everything becomes a little bit softer, less apocalyptic. No black and white. More middle. More pleasant."

"Well, that's great. I don't have a problem with you taking edibles," he told me.

"The other good news is—it's cut my drinking in half."

This was a sentence that I never expected to come out of my mouth, so I want to be very clear: I have no intention, now or in the future, of giving up alcohol. This isn't a book where I get sober at the end. However, cutting my drinking in half was an unexpected perk, and that is when I started to get serious about cannabis.

. . .

I had been approached by various weed companies to start my own line of cannabis products, but I didn't want to jump on the bandwagon until I had done due diligence and fully investigated what was available on the market. This meant that it became my job to know everything about every available oil, weed, candy, herb, and food item that contained cannabis.

I was sitting around my house in Los Angeles one weekend, with Glen and Shana, doling out the new edibles that I wanted them to try.

"Chelsea," Glen asked me, dripping in sarcasm. "Would you consider yourself a medical practitioner?"

"No, I think of myself as more of a pharmacological intuitive," I said, testing out the term in everyday usage. "I have a history of helping people, Glen, yourself included."

Glen and I both suffer from psoriasis, but only one of us had clear skin until I shared with Glen the prescription that had knocked it out of my system. Two doxycycline, twice a day, for ten days.* I gave the very same prescription to my hairstylist when she had a terrible bout of acne. Twice a day, ten days, never on an empty stomach. Glen no longer has psoriasis, and my hairstylist no longer has acne, and there are several African villagers who now have the cure to malaria.

My sister Simone is required to give formal presenta-

---

* Needless to say, I am not a doctor, nor can I examine you as you read this. So please don't follow these protocols as genuine medical advice that's meant for you. Use your head and see a real doctor.

tions at work, which makes her nervous. Her anxiety causes dry mouth, so I gave her a bottle of Propranalol, which is a beta-blocker that cuts off the signal from your neurotransmitters that tells your brain it's anxious.

"Thank God we have a doctor in the family," Simone said, after her second promotion.

My area of expertise isn't only limited to cannabis and pharmaceuticals. I have had a 100 percent success rate helping many women—friends who, prior to my intervention, hadn't gone number two in years—become regular. Women in particular struggle with regularity, so it is important to have bowel movement advocates out there. There are over-the-counter calcium magnesium pills called Mag O$_7$ from Aerobic Life, and if you start with four each night, typically by day three you will start to have regular bowel movements. At that point, I advise patients to reduce their intake to three pills in order to avoid morning diarrhea.

Breast inflammation before your period? Rose hips, once a day for a month. (Molly told me that one.)

Hangovers? Two Excedrin, and the headache will be gone in less than ten minutes. Caffeine is the antidote to headaches caused by alcohol, and Excedrin contains caffeine. If you've been drinking, milk thistle helps if you take it before you go to bed, but it's hard to remember to take something when you're shit-faced.

All in all, I've had an incredible track record with curing people, and the only mistakes I make are usually with myself, like the time I swallowed a yeast infection pill that was supposed to be administered vaginally—and then waited expectantly in the forty-eight hours that followed for a loaf of bread to pop out of my mouth.

I know if people have the personality for Xanax, or if they will do better on a lighter sleeping pill, like Sonata (generic brand is Zaleplon). I also know that Xanax isn't a sleeping pill, but that's what I use it for. Adderall is good for some people, but too much for certain personality types. High-energy people like myself do not need Adderall, no matter how tired you are, unless you want to wake up in the middle of the night cracking your knuckles. If you like Adderall, you should also look into Provigil or Nuvigil. That's what people in the government and the military use when they travel through different time zones. Provigil is the best thing I have ever taken for jet lag, or if I really need to focus. But again, if you have a knuckle-cracking problem, then you might want to start with a half. There is nothing I love more than getting on an international flight, popping a Xanax, and sleeping for twelve hours straight, but I have become so disgusted with the pharmaceutical industry in this country, I have redirected that passion and dedication into the healthier alternative—cannabis.

"Chelsea," Glen said, putting his fork down. "You should be a late-stage companion. That's something you could do. You're fun. Something activity-based, somewhere by the mountains, or a pool. Older men seem to be drawn to you, you'd get hired all the time."

"Who's in the late stage? Me or the companion?" I asked.

"The companion," Shana said, laughing. "Always the companion. You have a lot in common with older people."

"This can be the perfect foil for your identity crisis,

Chelsea. Since you can no longer date older guys, this is a way you can still hang out with them all the time." Glen wiped his mouth and took a sip of Mike's Hard Lemonade, which he had brought to my house. Glen and I are a lot alike. We find something we like, then abuse it for two months, and then we're on to the next thing. Glen was having a Mike's Hard Lemonade renaissance, and although I was repulsed, I understood it.

"Chelsea," Glen asked, "in your professional opinion, what procedure do you think Donald Trump is getting to make his face look like it does?"

"What do you mean?" I asked. "I don't think he's actually getting work done to look that bad. What he should be doing is resurfacing the texture of his skin, and at the very least, getting the fat sucked out from underneath his eyes. And maybe lipo, but he obviously can't even see clearly, if he thinks that what he's presenting is presentable. His ass is the size of Bert's—that should be first on his to-do list."

"You don't think he's doing stuff to his mouth?" Glen asked. He was being serious, so I looked up.

"Like what?"

"Is there some sort of surgical procedure or face treatment that makes your mouth look more like an anus?"

I had to think about that.

"I don't know anything about that. I mean, people usually make their lips bigger, not more anus-like."

"He may think that it looks good. It's as if his mouth keeps getting tighter and smaller."

I liked the idea of Donald Trump sewing his mouth closed, one surgical procedure at a time.

"This country has had a rough year." Glen sighed.

"Men have had a rough year," Shana said and laughed, looking at Glen.

"Well, you only have yourselves to blame. It's a wrap on old white men," I said.

"Yeah," Shana said, walking back to the table, a frozen ham in her hands. "Are you saving this for a special occasion?" She was definitely stoned if she wanted to cook a ham. I redirected my attention back to the only male in the room.

"Let me tell you a little story. Every week I go to the nail salon, where I get a massage on my forearms after my manicure. Getting a massage on my forearms is the closest thing I can relate to what getting a hand job must feel like. It's so specifically terrific, I could easily see myself climaxing at a nail salon, but I don't. That is the difference between men and women. We are more prone to controlling ourselves."

"Yes," Glen agreed, most women are. "But I would place you in the category of people who have trouble controlling themselves. It's a good thing you weren't born with male genitalia."

"I can guarantee that if I were, you would still never find me jerking off into a fucking plant."

"Who did that?" Glen asked, laughing.

"I don't know. One of those guys. Louis C.K. or Harvey Weinstein. One of them jerked off into a plant. I mean, seriously."

"Can you imagine jerking off into a plant?" Glen asked, disgusted. "What is wrong with everyone?"

"I'm stoned, high, drunk, and stoned," Shana said, with the frozen ham tucked into her armpit.

"You're not drunk," I reassured her, and guided her up-stairs to my bathroom, where I placed the frozen ham on the floor of the infrared sauna and told Shana it would be ready first thing in the morning.

"Is the sauna even on?" she asked.

"Yes," I told her as I guided her to my bed. "How do you feel?" I asked as we climbed into bed.

"Super warm and fuzzy," she told me. I got out my medical journal and made a note of her condition.

"And hungry?" I asked her. I had been working tirelessly on finding the right mixture of ingredients that didn't give you the munchies.

"Not really. The ham just reminded me of something Mom would have made at Christmas."

"Do you feel sad?" I asked her, taking out my medical notebook again.

"No, just warm and fuzzy," she repeated.

We lay in my bed, holding hands, looking out at the backyard lit by the lanterns hanging in the trees. I felt grateful in that moment that I was lying next to my sister, and for all the gifts life had given me, and for all the girls life had given me.

"I just want everything to go on forever," I told Shana, and then stuck my finger in her butt.

"When are we going to be too old to act like this?" she asked me, giggling.

"We'll never be too old to act like this," I reassured her.

Shana yawned. "Just because I get colonics, doesn't mean you can treat me like shit." Then she rolled over and fell asleep.

THE
YEAR
I BECAME
ME

I've never woken up feeling in danger. I've never woken up feeling like I didn't belong. I've woken up every day of my life thinking, *I've got the upper hand*—that I always had an avenue. I didn't know that was called privilege. I was too consumed with the things I still *didn't* have to think about what other people were missing.

Someone explained to me that for someone who's lived with privilege their whole life, equality feels like a loss. That made sense.

What would I be willing to give away in the name of equality? My house? My car? My career? What is my contribution?

No one likes to lose anything they've gotten comfortable with. Some people are more gracious, and some people have more experience with loss—and those people are usually either poor, of color, or marginalized because of their sexual preference or gender identity. If you're afraid of loss, you'll do anything to identify a variant; you'll seize on any reason to exclude an "other."

I was sitting in Dan's office one October morning telling him about the documentary I had started filming for Netflix on the subject of white privilege. I told him how on the very first day of shooting, I had already managed to offend a black girl by tapping her on the ass.

"So now Netflix is making me take racial-sensitivity classes," I said.

"Why did you tap a girl's ass?" Dan asked, with a furrowed brow.

"I don't know," I told him. "As a sign of affection? That's how I was intending it anyway. Like a girl thing. Like sisterhood." I moved my shoulders to demonstrate a shoulder bump, except no one was there to bump with.

"Okay," he said, sighing. "Isn't that what this documentary is all about, though? Pointing out to white people what they're doing wrong?"

"Or pointing out to me what I'm doing wrong. Jesus, do I feel stupid. Here I am, thinking I'm going to enlighten white people, and my lightbulb is out. Way out. I don't even know if I have a lightbulb. I've been grabbing people's asses for years. White and black. It's total privilege. Why do I think I can touch other people's bodies?"

"You've said yourself you have a lack of boundaries," Dan reminded me, and then he added for good measure, "Personally, I don't think it's normal to touch other people's bodies."

"Yeah, I got it," I said, throwing one hand up in the

form of a stop sign. "I think that just because I'm a girl, I expect other girls to know I'm not a threat and that I'm not trying to sexually assault anyone—but I've never taken into account what it means if you don't like to be touched, or you've been assaulted, or that many black women don't want to be defined by their hair or their asses. I have to retrain my brain. Just this morning I grabbed my cleaning lady's ass when she bent over to rub faces with Bert."

Dan was confused. "Who's Bert?"

"Ugh, it's not important," I told him. I wasn't going to sit there and talk to my therapist about the pangs of jealousy I had toward my cleaning lady and her relationship with my dog. Talk about privilege.

"It's the same thing with the #MeToo movement. I had no idea that one in three women have been sexually assaulted. How is it that I didn't know how rampant that was in the very industry I work in? How rampant it is in every industry. I feel like a member of the Catholic Church who just found out how prevalent child rape is among priests. Why did I assume my privileged experience was the typical experience and not the other way around?"

"I don't think you should beat yourself up for asking these questions. You should be grateful that you're now asking them."

"In my world there is no such thing as an invasion of privacy. Nothing's off-limits. I guess that speaks to my lack of empathy. Maybe I should think for a second about what other people's limits might be instead of assuming they have the same limits I do." I looked up. "This song is getting very old. Every time I feel like I'm getting a handle on this empathy thing, it keeps rearing its head."

"Well, before, you didn't even know you were missing it. You're thinking about it now, so that's progress. Identification. Awareness. Modification."

Feeling spoiled was a good head space for me to live in for a while. But it was also time to turn that feeling into something else.

"My question, though, is: Am I really interested in helping fight the good fight for the right reasons, or is it because misogyny and racism represent boundaries, and I resent boundaries? What are my motives? Am I really fighting for others, or am I fighting for myself?"

"Did you apologize to the girl whose ass you grabbed?"

"Yes!" I exclaimed.

"How did that feel?" he asked.

"Awesome," I told him. "I felt defensive at first, like I hadn't done anything worth apologizing for, but I recognized that it wasn't about my intention; it was about how my action was received. That my action was unwelcome. I get that now, and it didn't take long for it to click this time."

"That's empathy—"

"Oh!" I blurted out, interrupting Dan.

"What?"

"My dad died." I put down my iced tea and threw up my hands. "I'm sorry. I totally forgot to tell you."

Dan very uncharacteristically jolted forward in his chair, with his hands folded, nonplussed. I use the word "nonplussed" because it means two things: very surprised or not surprised at all—*almost* as if a vet came up with its two definitions. Dan was surprised.

To be fair, it was quite a predictable reaction for anyone to have, which is probably the reason I forgot to tell him. My plan was to tell no one about my dad dying—except maybe Mary.

"When did this happen?" he asked, alarmed.

"Sunday. I was on my way back from canvassing in Orange County."

"I'm so sorry." Dan's face was filled with so much sympathy, I felt as if I would end up comforting him.

"It's okay. I'm okay." I stared at him. Nothing was going to come out in the way of tears. I felt devoid of feelings, nothing even closely related to grief.

"I don't really feel anything," I told Dan. "I mean, we're halfway through our session and I just remembered, so . . ." I looked at him, searching for an answer—preferably from him. He was still leaning forward in his chair, but had relaxed a little.

"Well, your brain is used to wrapping up death and putting it away."

"But after all this work we've done, am I just repeating the only way I know? What if I'm not growing at all?" I sat in my chair across from Dan, wondering what to say next.

"Honestly, I was more upset when Chunk died. That seems fucked-up."

"Well, dogs are pretty good at not disappointing you, and loving you unconditionally."

"Not Bert."

"Who is this *Bert*?" he asked for the second time, slightly irritated.

"He's a stuffed animal I have at home," I told him, dismissively, and got back to business. "Do you think I'm in denial, because it doesn't feel that way, but I want to know if this is going to be another case of delayed grief. It feels like I've already mourned my father while he was alive. I haven't told anyone yet. I mean, Molly, Karen, and Brandon know because they know all things, but I haven't even told Mary."

"Why not?"

"I don't want that kind of attention."

"You may not want it, but what if you are ready to receive it?"

"I'm not going to use my father's death to mourn my brother, if that's what you're asking." I felt like I had finally grieved my brother too, and although I felt sad at the finality of my father's death, I wasn't sad he was gone. I was relieved.

. . .

Glen and I had driven to see my dad in Pennsylvania a month before he died, and my dad was a shell of himself—it was no way for anyone to live. He had shrunk from his king-size, larger-than-life self into a little old man in a wheelchair—white as a ghost, his once gargantuan hands now frail, reduced to half their size, with the veins on his hands so prominent that they looked like the hands of an old lady. We brought him some pizza, which we fed to him slowly in order to prevent him from swallowing it whole, and before we left, I rubbed lotion on his head, something my dad has loved for years—head jobs. My dad was weak and slow to speak, telling us the same thing he had been saying for years—that he was working on a book about my mother. He may have been working on a book about my mother, but it would have been only in his head. He hadn't picked up a pen in years, and in my father's mind, typing was for girls.

"You know," Glen said, when we were pulling away from my dad's nursing home, "you only have yourself to thank for forcing him to get that quintuple-bypass surgery years ago."

"That's nice, thank you. I was young and stupid back then. I thought I was saving our family."

"At least then he could have gone out on a high note," Glen added.

"Yeah, I got it, Glen. Wouldn't it be so much more humane if we could just put him down?" I said. "You need to put me down when things go south. I don't want to fight cancer or anything like that. I'm wiped out. I'm fine to leave this life early."

Glen's youngest son was in the backseat and said, "I'll put you down," and then asked if we could stop for candy.

"There's no reason my life shouldn't end by the hands of a Russian," I told little Teddy, as I looked out the window at the bleak New Jersey landscape. "That would make the most sense for me at this current point in time. That would be a complete 360." We stopped at a 7-Eleven, and Teddy and I went inside to fill up on candy that he could devour before we arrived back at Glen's home, which everyone in our family refers to as the Russian embassy.

I was leaving for Bali the next day and asked Glen what the protocol was if my dad died while I was halfway around the world.

"Well, typically, Chelsea, people come home for their father's funeral."

"Copy that," I told him, and turned up the music.

• • •

I told Dan that I didn't want people calling and telling me how sorry they were about my dad, because I still had a hard time accepting any pity. Especially now, since I wasn't even that torn up about it.

"It just feels fraudulent."

"Will there be a funeral?" Dan asked me.

"It's this Sunday, in New Jersey. We're keeping it low-key."

"Okay, so, just so you know," Dan explained to me, in a very kindergarten-teacher kind of way, "things may come up for you when you go home."

"Uh-huh."

"So, you can call me anytime if you need to talk."

I couldn't imagine myself calling Dan from my father's funeral, but I appreciated the crossing of boundaries. Crossing boundaries meant love.

• • •

My dad's funeral was one of those instances when you're reminded of what it means to show up for people. The tradition. The absolute wretched grayness of a day like that. Why do people show up—if not out of decency, and tradition?

There were maybe thirty of us, all related in one way or another, gathered at his grave on a cold fall day in New Jersey. Everyone reminisced about what a character he was, how he had such a huge personality, and they all talked about how much he loved my mother. *Your father was so in love with Ritala.* "Ritala" was the moniker my father gave to my mother, in that singsong kind of way they talked when they were flirting with each other, or when they were being playful with us. Every person at the funeral also sang her name the way my father always did. "Ri-ta-la."

It was as pleasant a funeral as I could have ever imagined for my father. I talked to his cousins and other relatives who had known him his whole life, and was reminded that he had a life before I came into it. His cousin Jerry had seen him two weeks earlier at his nursing home, and had brought him a corned beef sandwich. I thanked her for doing that and then realized how strange it was for me to thank her for spending time with the cousin she had known long before I came on the scene. I asked her what it was like to grow up with him.

"Well, his mother was crazy," said Jerry, who'd grown up across the street from him. "She must have been bipolar, or something. Your dad was the baby, and she spoiled him rotten. All the girls on Tracy Avenue loved Seymour."

Another cousin, Linda, said my dad was the first person to the hospital when she was sick with cancer. That he visited her repeatedly, and would stay for hours. Her daughter told me he was the first person to the hospital when she had a baby. Linda told me about a time ten years earlier when my dad had picked up her sister and her to go to lunch. She said that he pulled over on the side of the road to urinate, and that she and her sister were appalled.

"After your mom died, that was it for him," she said. I wanted to tell her that my dad had been urinating on the side of the road long before my mother died, but reminded myself I no longer needed to button every conversation with something funny. I reminded myself to sit, and listen, and not fill the air up with noise just because someone else stopped talking.

Glen gave a eulogy. He had done this at Chet's funeral and at my mom's funeral, but this was the one he had the most difficult time getting through. I had never seen Glen become so undone; he is usually stoic and filled to the brim with sarcasm, so it was painful to see him struggling, and I wondered what it meant for him—all the memories he had of my father that I didn't know about.

When everyone was done speaking, Roy, Glen, Simone, Shana, and I were staring over my mom's and Chet's headstones and my dad's freshly dug grave.

Five against three. The next person who dies, we'll be even.

Even in death, I was keeping score.

That's when I caught myself. *Stop.*

. . .

I reminded myself to focus not on the end of someone's life but on the whole, and to look at my dad's life the way he would want me to see it.

My sisters had put together photo albums of my dad when he was young. Pictures of him as a baby, as a teenager, of him traveling through Europe, or living in Mexico, where he dreamed of becoming a writer. As a young father, always with that great big smile and waving with his great big hands. A reminder to never stop smiling, to hold on to happiness, and to find joy. To always wag your tail. Be playful. To live life with your leg kicked out.

The funeral was a reminder to look for the youth in a person, rather than their age. To look at their hopes and dreams, and the family they created, and their best moments with that family. To see them when they were filled with hope—not when the rug was pulled out from under them. To remember that death should be a reminder of all the memories of that person at their best, and the best private moments you shared with that person. All the stories and the photographs painted a picture of my father I hadn't known. Why did I seem surprised at the amount of time he spent with the boys and the pictures of all their road trips and summers on the beach? I had those moments with him too—something I had seemed to have let dim in memory, replaced by yelling and fighting, and all the times when we were broke or he hadn't sold a car in months, or the times my mother had to work because he had zero financial stability. (Another example of unconscious privilege—assuming that mothers shouldn't have to work.) There were also good things to hold on to, yet I had been choosing to let the bad outweigh the good and judge someone by how they behaved when they were at their lowest.

Effusive, smiling bright. He even dressed well before I was born. He was so handsome on the beach with two kids, then three, then four, then five, then six. Then five again. There were pictures of him long after Chet died where he was smiling again. He had aged significantly, he'd let himself go, but there were pictures of us holding hands, hugging, and laughing—I had forgotten about that.

• • •

"I think my dad was an eight," I told Dan, the Monday morning after the funeral.

"Yeah, maybe he was." Dan smiled. "We can try to figure it out, if you want."

I didn't. Dan and I hadn't talked about the Enneagram in a while, and at that point it felt like the Enneagram—or Dan's interpretation of it—was just the framework I needed in order to address my issues head-on.

"Guess who else is an eight?" I asked Dan.

"Who?"

"Donald Trump."

"Oh, yes, I've heard that." He gave a small laugh.

"That would have been nice to open with, Dan," I told him, sternly. "My father, Donald Trump, and I are all number eights. What . . . a thruple."

"What's a thruple?" Dan asked.

"Oh, and also . . ." I remembered. "A lot of eights are sociopaths. I mean, for fuck's sake, Dan."

"You are not a sociopath," Dan said, very slowly. A little too slowly, if you ask me.

Dan explained there are self-actualized eights, who are able to identify their weaknesses and growth edges and are very different from unactualized eights.

"You are becoming self-actualized. Now maybe you can have a little more empathy for your father, knowing he was also in a lot of pain. And that, if he was an eight, maybe he too lacked empathy." That made sense. My father lacked empathy, for sure.

I liked the idea of blaming my eightness on my father, but I had come too far with Dan for that to be my mental footprint. Instead, I remembered all the pictures of my father as a young boy, growing up in Newark, New Jersey. Running on the beach with my three brothers, with a football in hand. With his huge smile, and these great big lips—he looked like a hurricane of life. I was going to remember my dad the way he would have wanted to be remembered—at his peaks.

"People have been dropping like flies," I said to Dan. "Every time I look up, there's a missed call. Tammy, Chunk, my cousin, my father. It's all so strange. This year feels like a dream. The first time I start really dealing with my grief about Chet, it feels like death is knocking on my door. I keep losing things that I love, and I now know what people mean when they say they've had a rough year."

"Do you feel like you are grieving?"

I didn't, and needed to explain to Dan what years of walking around with psychological cement felt like.

"I have a very out-of-sight, out-of-mind attitude when it comes to people. It seems harsh, but I really just stop thinking about people once a relationship has been severed."

"Well, that's the way you say goodbye to people. It has to be black or white. That's the only way you know."

"I don't miss people. Ever. I don't think I'll miss my dad."

"You've been preventing yourself from missing people because missing someone means that you are vulnerable, and you are only just learning how to be vulnerable. You can't expect these things to shift overnight. You are trying very hard."

"Yeah," I said, sighing. "You keep saying that."

"Are you angry?" Dan asked me.

"No. Nothing even close to angry."

"Are you sad?"

"Um, I want to say yes, but I feel like that would be a lie. I guess, based on my reaction to his death, my father wasn't one of my self-defining relationships."

"Maybe he wasn't," Dan agreed.

"*That's* sad," I told him, with the tears finally welling up in my eyes.

I felt sad, but not necessarily about my father. What I was mourning wasn't just my brother, or my father, or my cousin, or Chunk, or Tammy. I was mourning the childhood that had lasted years into my adulthood—because I got stuck. I was reconciling myself to the loss of my youth as a self-actualized adult, now that I had the tools to face it all—and now that I was officially an orphan, and had no choice but to grow up.

"I totally get me now," I told Dan. "I can work with this."

. . .

I've learned that many people are just bridges to someone else. Some people become bridges that you take back and forth to get back to yourself. That's how I interpret self-defining relationships. The people who bring you back to you. The ones who say, "You are always welcome here. You are family. I love you, and there's nothing you can do about it, so get used to it." My father's funeral was a reminder of how important family is, and how important tradition is. That showing up for a funeral is tradition, and that tradition is not a trope and that there's nothing stale about it. Every person that came to my father's funeral had given me information I hadn't had before—information I was now willing to receive. My dad would have loved that.

There are a lot of people in my life who I know love me and care about me and worry about me, but before Dan, I was intent on tuning out that noise. I would shudder or turn away because the last thing I wanted to feel was safe. That feeling had backfired on me before, and it took me thirty years to figure that out.

I didn't know about attachment figures before I met Dan. I couldn't see that I'd adopted certain habits to avoid my deep pain. I cultivated a kind of hubris that allowed me to barrel through life, knocking over everything in my way, and then look back and be surprised at all the casualties. Casualties represented weakness, or disloyalty, or people who couldn't cut the mustard. I never took them as signs that maybe the common denominator was me. Chet had basically commandeered most of my life, and I barely knew the guy.

Don't let other people decide what kind of mood you're going to be in. Don't let anyone change your life in one day. Don't let death take you down and keep you down. Go down, but get back up. If we don't give in to our despair—and instead lock it away—we fail to properly mourn the people we love. How on earth are we honoring the very people we are grieving if we fail to mourn them fully? We should be celebrating the people we've lost. I missed thirty years of celebrating my brother.

. . .

I was no longer shipwrecked. I was now floating somewhere in Katama Bay—the bay of water that is filled with my favorite childhood memories, the bay that separates Chappaquiddick from Edgartown—thinking about how strong I feel with my new set of tools. By sheer force of will, I can get myself almost anywhere I'd like to go, but I choose to use my newly acquired awareness as a strength—a tool to keep me in place—and not as part of my kinetic motion. I know I can continue swimming away from myself, or I can get out of the water and stand on my own two feet, firmly in one place, and take a look at all the other people struggling to stay afloat. I have the strength and mental grit to withstand what comes my way, and if someone I love dies along the way, I will survive.

What matters the most is that I was ready to take an uncomfortable look at myself and ready to accept whatever image I saw. I'd like to think that the messenger—Dan—had something to do with it. Maybe it's as much about the messenger as it is the message. I needed Dan, and I needed the message. He could have delivered that message in a Magic 8-Ball. I had found someone I was ready to dig deep with.

Once Dan elucidated all my attachment issues in relation to Chet, I made it my business to unlock my nine-year-old brain and take a look at my behavior. That's when the lights started turning on everywhere I looked. Chet's death and my response to it became the blueprint I followed anytime I experienced disappointment with people. I terminated friendships, with little sentimentality, because that was how I thought relationships ended. You move on and forget about that person in your life. Keep moving. There are new people everywhere.

I learned that adventure is never bad, but the alacrity with which you go through life has an impact on the wisdom that life has to offer you. That slowing down doesn't

mean you have to do less. It means you have to pay attention more and catch what the world is throwing at you.
That every situation you put yourself in deserves your full
attention, and that each of us has a responsibility to be
more aware of ourselves and of others.

I learned that saying nothing can be much more powerful than saying anything. To not work so hard at making an
impression and to let things settle more. Some people's
lessons are to learn how to use their voice, or to speak out
more. My lesson is to keep quiet a little more and let things
happen around me instead of always inserting myself. It
used to be hard not to say the thing that I believed would
change a person forever, and it's now so easy to say nothing. There's power in adjusting your behavior and pulling
back. No more screeching or waving my arms around to
get attention. I've always been more interested in sharing
what I was thinking, but now I try to think about what I'm
thinking.

I have confidence in my ability to make the best out of
a bad situation. I have an equal amount of confidence in
myself to make the worst out of a mediocre situation.
When left in a gray area or anything that could be con-
strued as average, I will always tug in one direction or another. Far left or far right—that is my habit. Now that I
have identified my propensity to do that, it's up to me to
identify when that response is appropriate and when it's
appropriate to look for some gray. Not everything has to be
so definitive.

I also know when I need to allow myself to cry. I don't
fight it as much. I know if I'm tired, I'm going to be more

sensitive; if I'm exhausted, I will have less patience. When I'm impatient, it's because of me and my mental state and not somebody else's fault, and I catch myself. Identify that you are going through something and go through it. Know it. Don't push fast-forward. Know that if you are sad or upset, it's for a reason, and then reason with yourself. Don't try to please everyone. Be honest. Know the situation. Identification. Awareness. Modification.

Strength doesn't have to eclipse vulnerability. Vulnerability is strength. Being able to apologize is strength. I haven't yet nailed that, but I'm getting there, and the most important thing isn't always the giant leap, it's the steps you take to get where you want to go. I had to run miles around what I perceived to be strength in order to find real strength, and come back stronger.

I thought I was nailing it, for a really long time.

I spent my twenties wanting people to think I was great.

I spent my thirties thinking people thought I *was* great.

I turned forty, and I started wondering what I thought about me.

• • •

I was starting to feel less desultory about the state of the country. I was starting to feel purposeful. I knew the impact my words could have. That my heart was in the right place for compassion and understanding, and that the act of helping people simply because you were born in the right country was and is necessary.

I talked to Dan about my desire to work for a better cause and the feelings of insecurity that came along with that. Would I be able to wait and see what would happen without instant results? In 2018, I had thrown myself fully and wholly into getting women elected and getting minorities and marginalized groups represented in government—and getting all of the above registered to vote. I knew from previous experiences that if I dove headfirst into something, results would follow.

I couldn't read enough or learn enough about elections, about government, about what it takes to run for office. (Not much, it turns out.)

I wanted Donald Trump to be erased from history—although I understand that not to be possible. Generations after us will have to learn about how badly we chose and how long we allowed it to go on for.

A dictator is usually homegrown. Someone who has been spoiled and coddled their whole life and has never really done a single thing of merit. Narcissism at its finest.

Donald Trump is a crustacean. He is a bag of psychological cement that was the catalyst for me unlocking my own bag of psychological cement, and for this I am grateful. Would I go back to the way I was and live the rest of my life like that, if it meant avoiding Donald Trump altogether? In a heartbeat.

I know now how small I am, and how big the world is. I know that the entire democracy of America is in the hands of each person who holds the right to vote. I know now that it is not only about using your singular voice, however big or small your platform is, but about helping everyone and encouraging every person to do the same. You may cast a small net, but every small net adds up to something bigger.

I may not be able to save the world, but I can save people. One by one, family by family, and that is worthwhile. Helping people understand how important their voice is. That getting involved in politics is worthwhile, and doesn't have to be your whole life. That too many people before us have fought to earn us the right to vote, and not to exercise that right is disrespectful to those who devoted their lives to seeking justice and fairness for all. They weren't just fighting for themselves; they fought for all of us. We must all fight together. To be strong together. To fight not only for the rights that affect you. We have a duty to fight for the rights that affect all of our brothers and sisters. Stand for something. Say something. Stick your neck out and be brave. Fight. In 2018 we elected 116 women to Congress, because so many people fought so tirelessly.

Your voice has meaning. Find something you care about that has nothing to do with you, and learn about it. Pay attention when you're tired. Take care of yourself. Read more. Watch less TV. Find new people to teach you their life lessons. Be proactive.

Know that you have something of value that is unlike what anyone else has.

The world is only getting browner and gayer, and if you don't hop on board, you're going to miss the bus.

Go after happiness like it is the only thing you can take with you when you die. Stand up for yourself. Treat yourself the way you treat the person you love most in the world. Get on your own team.

Wake up. Take a nap. Laugh. Cry. Rinse. Repeat.

ACKNOWLEDGMENTS

Many thanks to Mengfei Chen, Greg Mollica, Kelly Chian, and Debbie Glasserman. Thank you to Dan Siegel for helping me put my head on straight. Thanks to all the B's in my life: Brandon, Bitchie, Bitch, Bebz, Ben, Bert, and Bernice. Molly, my sisters and brothers, my cousins, to Terry and Gaby, and to all my buddies. You know who you are. And to Michael Morris for coming up with the title. To my editor, Julie Grau, who knew I was capable of writing something deeper than I had before—and encouraged me to let it all out. This was the best writing experience I've had and I'm grateful you pushed me in the right direction: truth.

ABOUT THE AUTHOR

CHELSEA HANDLER is a writer, comedian, producer, TV host, activist, and the author of five consecutive *New York Times* bestsellers. She hosted the late-night talk show *Chelsea Lately* on the E! network from 2007 to 2014, and released a documentary series, *Chelsea Does,* on Netflix in January 2016. In 2016 and 2017, Handler hosted the talk show *Chelsea* on Netflix. She is at work on a documentary about white privilege that will be released by Netflix in 2019.

chelseahandler.com
Facebook.com/chelseahandler
Twitter: @chelseahandler
Instagram: @chelseahandler
Snapchat: @chelseahandler